J A Ellwood BSc(Econ),MCIPD

Management Tips and Tales

Essential reading for all managers
— a briefcase browser

Published by 3E Publications

First published in the United Kingdom in 2005

With special thanks to Tony Kay and Pat Wordley

3e Training Ltd provides specialist interactive training for individuals and groups who wish to improve their communication, training and coaching skills.

Contact
3e Publications / 3e Training Ltd
20 Redmayne Drive
Carnforth
Lancs
LA5 9XA

Email: john3e@aol.com

ISBN 0-9524203-1-7

CONTENTS

Training

Workshops

Presenting

Team Briefing

The Four Pillars of Confidence

When presenting, facilitating, coaching or taking part in intervie
confidence is enhanced by good preparation and self-contro

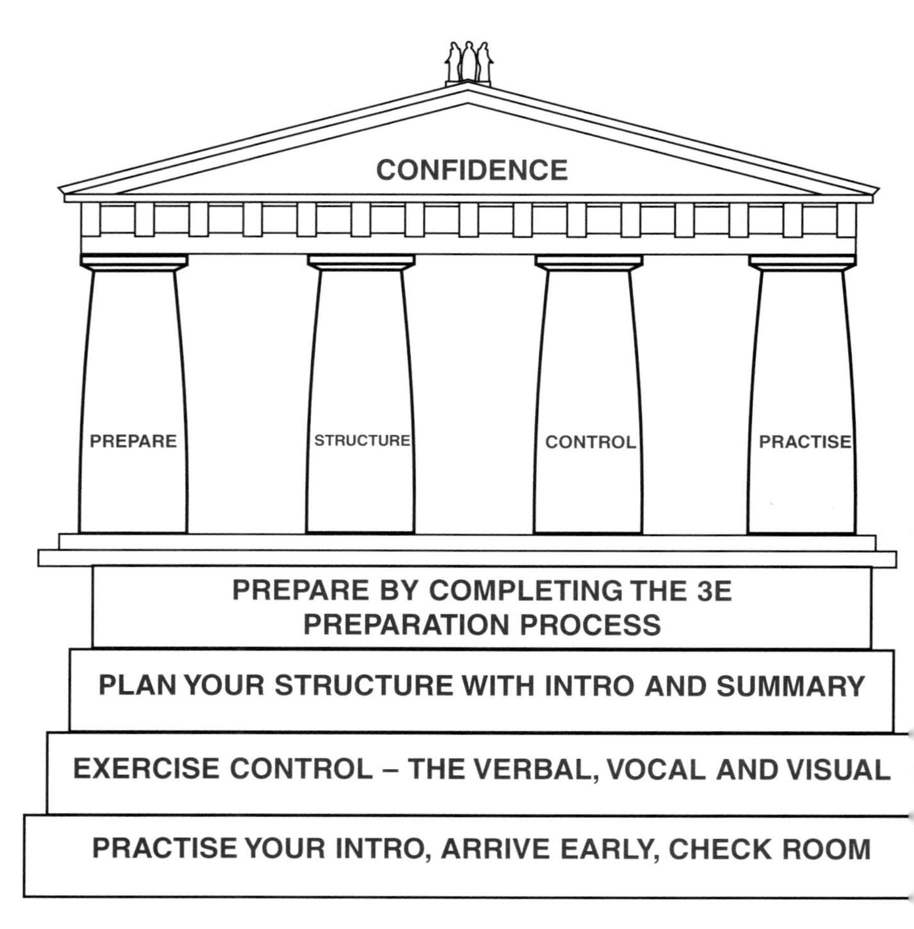

"Orators are made, not born"

Preparation
The 3E Presentation Process

low these 10 steps when preparing a sentation or workshop.

ep 1. Consider your audience

'hat's in it for them?

e clear about the benefits your audience can expect to gain.

'hat is their existing knowledge?

'hat are their backgrounds?

ow many are likely to attend?

'ho are the decision makers?

'hat are their names, roles, job titles?

ow receptive will they be?

ep 2. Define the purpose

re you there to persuade or inform?

larify your goal in one short sentence.

.g. "*To persuade Telecom plc to invest in our new billing system*".

To update Universal Utilities on the progress of our system upgrade".

you seek to persuade you will need a section about benefits.

well defined purpose will indicate the key points that need to

e clear in each section of the presentation.

:akes me five minutes to prepare a two hour speech two hours to prepare a five minute speech"

ston Churchill.

Step 3. List your 3-4 section titles

For example:

To Persuade	**To Inform**
INTRO	**INTRO**
PAIN - What is the problem	Progress to date
PROPOSAL - What we can do	Outstanding issues
PROFIT - How you will benefit	Next steps
PROOF - Why we are confident of success	**SUMMARY**
SUMMARY	

Step 4. Consider possible questions

Will you have the chance to cover all they need to know?

Should you amend the structure to include more about resources, cost, timescales etc?

Do you need help from elsewhere?

Ask yourself questions based on: WHAT and WHY and WHEN
HOW and WHERE and WHO

Step 5. Identify key points

Do not yet consider the introduction and summary.

What 4-5 key points are essential in each section?

Distinguish between what they must know and what is nice to know

These points can be transferred to your prompt cards.

Step 6. Consider the timing

In a typical presentation, you will need at least a minute for your INTRO and about 1/2 minute for your SUMMARY.

Decide which of your sections requires the longest time.

Remember that audience participation is an excellent method but can eat away at your time.

Step 7. How the key points will be supported

w are you going to keep the audience engaged?
werPoint is usually very badly used.
'e your power away to supporting material cautiously.
werPoint should not be a prompt, a crutch or a distraction.
oid boring text slides.
nsider PowerPoint for pictures, charts, graphs etc.

ernatives to PowerPoint

- u
- amples
- ops
- dience participation
- ımour (not jokes)
- colleague
- emonstration
- exercise
- Stories
- Current affairs
- Video/DVD
- Flip chart
- Audio tape/CD
- Music
- Quiz
- Stimulating the imagination

Step 8. Prepare prompt cards

e one card per section.
ep the number of words used per card to a minimum (e.g. max 10).
e coloured pens and highlighters to make the cards attractive.
e act of preparing cards will help to trigger your memory.
yourself HOW to deliver as well as WHAT to deliver.

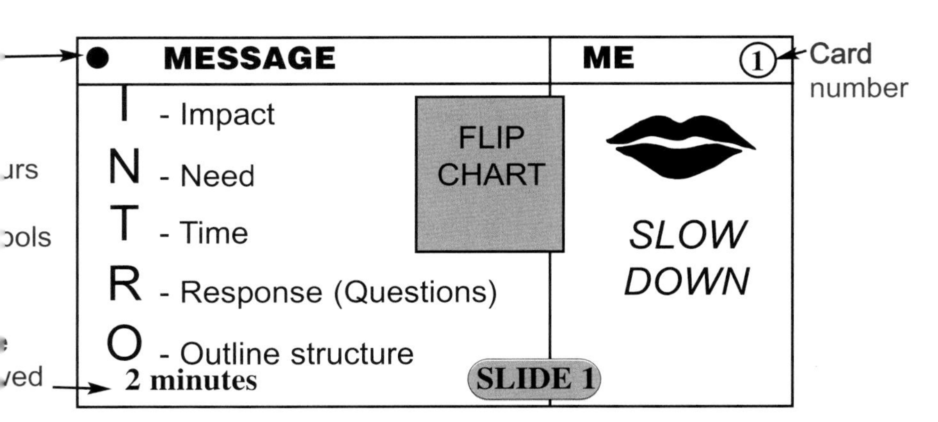

Step 9. Prepare your materials

Remember to use PowerPoint only if it adds value.

When in PowerPoint slideshow, use the **B key** to blank the screen.

Collect and check your props, aids and other material and decide where they will be placed in the room.

Check equipment. Have back-up and spares if necessary.

Avoid cluttering your delivery space.

Step 10. Consider your action points

How will you improve your delivery? e.g. Pause, Pace, Eye Contact, Positi

Work on at least one improvement every time you present.

Arrive early and manage the room

Eliminate distractions:

- Windows
- Pictures
- Paintings
- Noises
- Bright light
- Barriers
- Smells
- Temperature

Create a welcoming atmosphere:

- Seating
- Visibility
- Tidy
- Clear directions

Decide on the place for your PowerPresence (the star ★ position).

Find out who can help with equipment, power, refreshments, fire alarms, ex parking etc.

Begin with the INTRO

/our introduction includes the following, it will always succeed.

Impact	Begin with something to raise expectations. Do not say "Hello, my name is..." Consider interaction, a story, a prop, a picture, current affairs.
Need	Remind the audience of their reason to listen - perhaps a key benefit.
Time	Tell them the duration.
Response	Tell the audience what response you want . i.e. when will questions be appropriate.
Outline	Outline your structure so the audience knows what to expect.

: INTRO can be in any order, but always seek to begin with impact.
er your Impact, you may or may not need to give your name.

End with a summary

summary will typically last for half to one minute.
hould include a sentence or phrase about each section and must refer
our top 3-4 key points.
s the case for every section, the summary should be clearly identifiable
begin by saying "In summary..." or similar.
not introduce any new material.
nk the audience for their time.
e questions.

First and last is remembered

s been demonstrated that the first and last parts of a speech are the
s most likely to be remembered. It is essential therefore to develop
rehearse well-planned INTROs and Summaries.

When Using PowerPoint

Do not	Do
Use PowerPoint as your prompts	Use pictures and interesting images
Use bullet points	Blank the images by using the B key
Use animation	Consider that text slides may be a useful handout but not of use during the presentation
Read off the slides	Think about using some slides in an interactive way to stimulate discussion
Have slides permanently displayed	Control what you want to be the focus of attention — do not let PowerPoint compete with you, nor you with PowerPoint
Use slides because everyone else uses them	
Start with a slide showing your name	
BE A PowerPoint SLAVE	**MASTER THE MEDIUM**

"The best effort of a fine person is felt after we hav left their presence"
Ralph Waldo Emerson

"Presence is more than just being there".
Malcolm Forbes

Words that must never be used in presentations, workshops or training

Fillers

Erm, Um
Basically
Absolutely
Like
Reality
The reality is
Clearly
Well...
Cool
At the end of the day
In terms of...
Actually
Actual
Essentially
OK
You know
To be honest
So...
Right
Just
At this moment in time
In essence...

Submissive words

Boring
Hope
May I...
If you'll bear with me...
Sorry
Complicated
Try
I would like...
Graveyard shift
Technical

Clichés and Trendy Jargon

Climate change
Utilisation
Go the extra mile
Oh My God!
Downsizing
Rightsizing
Plain vanilla
Perfect
Diversity
Paradigm
Give110%
Doh!
Delayering
Synergy
...is key

problem with these words is that they become meaningless, sloppy, lazy distracting: They also can betray a lack of certainty.

The solution is regular PowerPauses.

The 3E Presentation Process

1. Audience:		10. Personal Actions:	
2. Purpose:			
3. Structure	**5. Key Points**	**6. Time**	**7. Support/Engage**
INTRO	IMPACT: NEED: TIME: RESPONSE: OUTLINE:		
Title Section 1			
Title Section 2			
Title Section 3			
Title Section 4			
Summary			
4. Likely Questions:			**8. Prepare cards**
			9. Prepare Support

Fail to prepare, prepare to fail!

Think of your presentation as an iceberg. Your spectacular delivery is supported by the depth of your preparation.

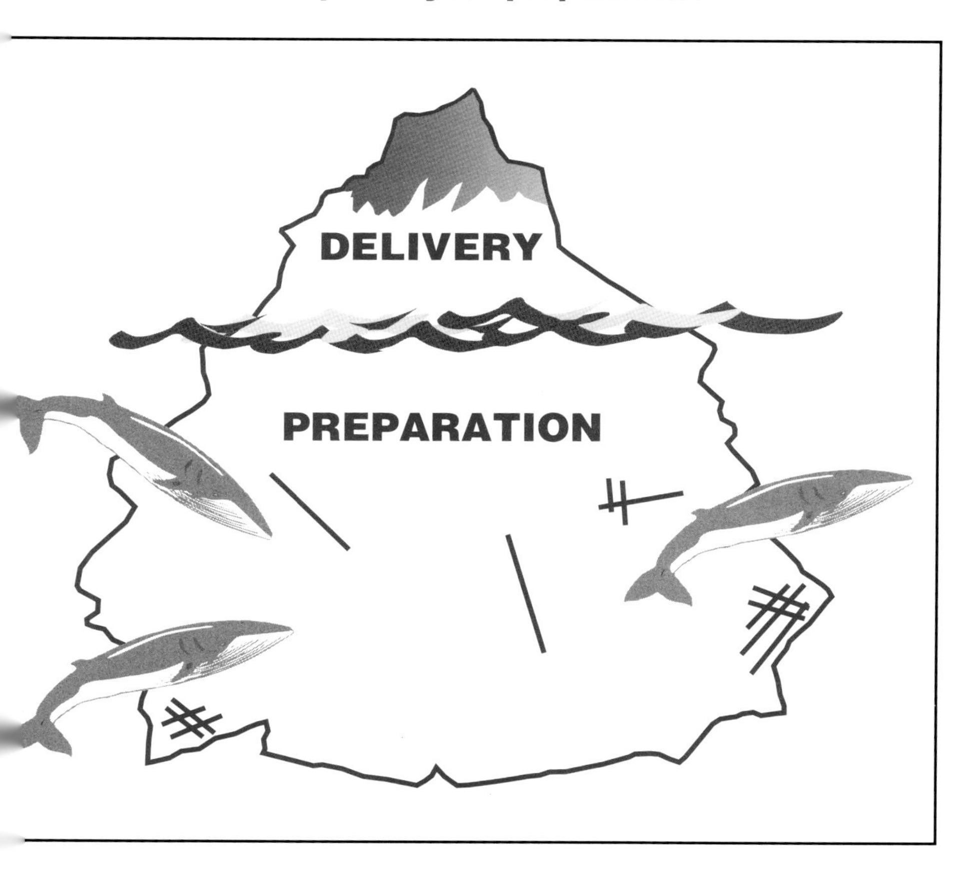

· sorry this letter is so long,
·l not have the time to write a shorter one" -
Shaw.

Linking the Sections

Prepare to link the different parts of your talk. Let the audience know where you/they are and where you are going.

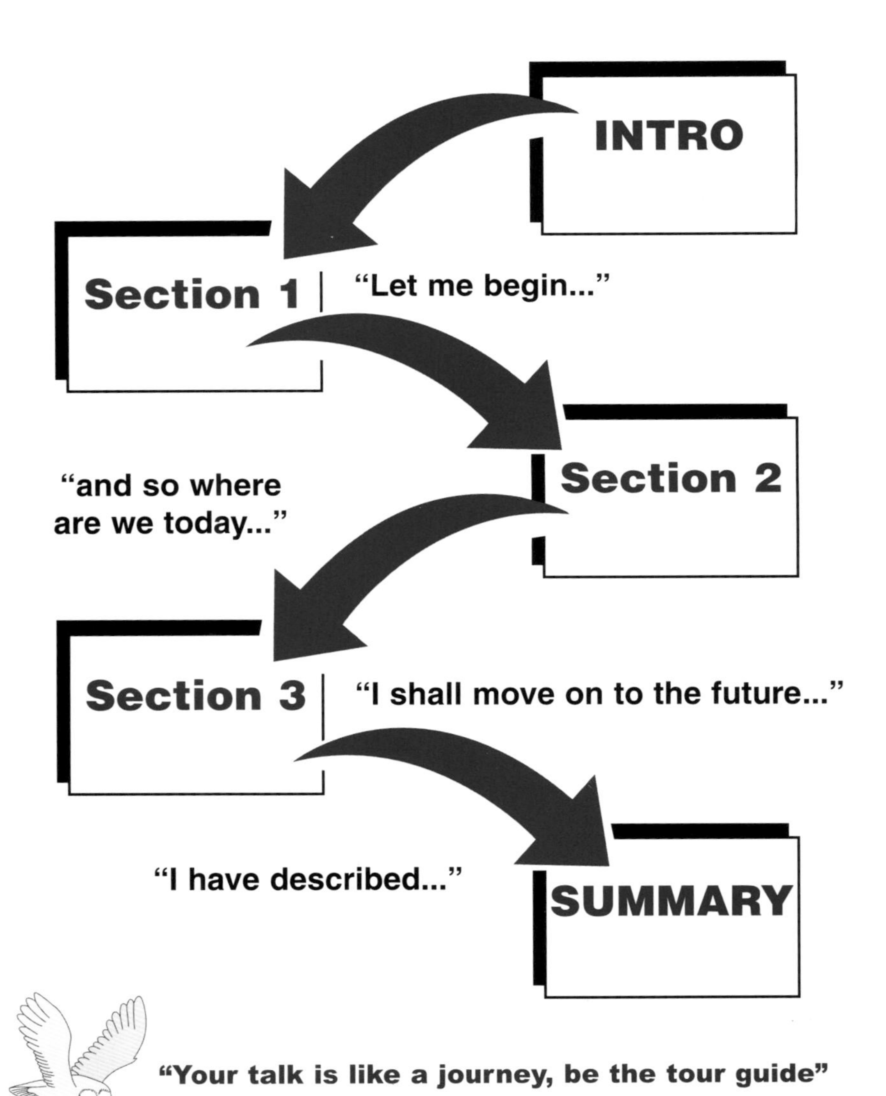

"Your talk is like a journey, be the tour guide"

Preparing Yourself

ıat you must do ......

there early.

aware that members of the audience may be observing you as you k your car. You only get one chance to make a first impression.

oduce yourself to as many people as possible.

lcome individuals by looking them in the eye, smiling and shaking ir hand.

k professional and composed.

to relax - *Breathe deeply.*
Roll your neck, tense, then release muscles.
Dress smartly, but comfortably.
Have an early night.

positive and show enthusiasm to all.

ȷage in conversation.

to remember first names.

nind yourself that you cannot fail if you have completed the '3E sentation Process'

at you must tell yourself ......

ıall succeed.
n in complete control.
I will enjoy myself.
The audience is friendly.

t impressions last. People make judgements within seconds of ing you.

ɣness has a strange element of narcissism, a ef that how we look, how we perform, is truly ortant to other people." - Andre Dubus.

Maintain Control and Manage Focu

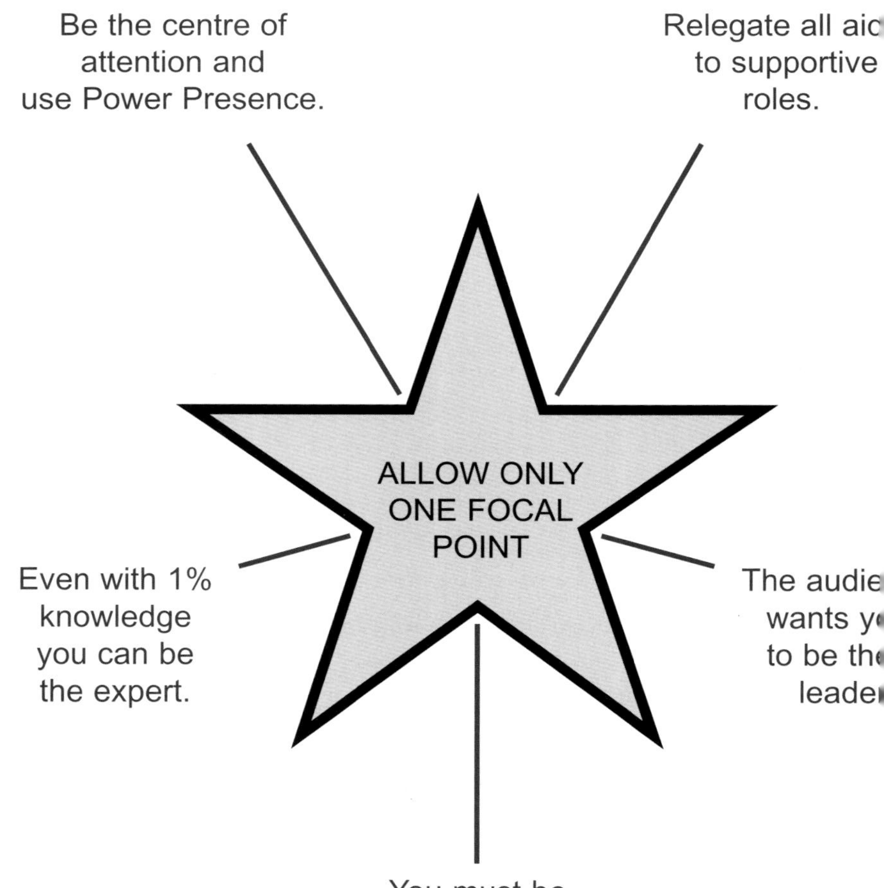

"Remember that you are the most important visua aid"

Behaviour

be most effective in dealing with people, we must control our haviour. For reasons of nature and nurture, we have an everyday style t may not be the best style to help us get what we want.

change our style we need to escape our comfort zone. This can be y hard. However, most people can adjust and choose a suitable haviour through practice and perseverance.

ou feel stuck with your "personality", try to develop by making small ryday changes: e.g. smile more often at people you meet; talk more wly when you are with friends or colleagues; adopt an improved ture when you walk.

nsider the behaviour listed on the following pages and think which nents you can develop to help you to influence people. (Submissive Aggressive behaviour is sometimes necessary to achieve your goals it is not behaviour that should be developed as the norm).

"Behaviour Breeds Behaviour"

gance of language may not be in the power of all s; but simplicity and straight forwardness are. e much as you would speak; speak as you think. ith your inferior, speak no coarser than usual; if your superiors, no finer. Be what you say; and, in the rules of prudence, say what you are" - Alford.

SUBMISSIVE	AGGRESSIVE
Unhelpful Verbal behaviour - what we shouldn't say	
"Erm", "basically", "you know", just...	Swear words
"May I..., If you don't mind..."	Denigration
"Sorry"	Put down
Boring, technical, complicated...	Racist, sexist etc, remarks
"I've been told to tell you..."	Tasteless jokes
"Hope, hopefully, try..."	Jargon, acronyms
Lots of detail	Lots of detail
Waffle	"you... will, do..."
Agrees with everyone	Disagree with everyone
One way - no feedback wanted	One way - no feedback allowed
Scripted	Scripted
Does not encourage questions	Sarcasm
	Asks intimidating questions
Unhelpful Vocal behaviour - how we shouldn't say it	
Too quiet	Too loud - ranting
Trailing off...poor enunciation	Monotone
Monotone	Indistinct
Too fast - let's get it over with	Too fast - listen or else
No pauses	No pauses
Unhelpful Visual behaviour - how we shouldn't look	
A soft touch - no impact on arrival	Full of bombast and bluster
No or little eye contact	Staring and glaring
Arms hidden or dangling	Arms folded - pointing fingers
Too far away from individual or group	Too close - invading personal space
Slouching	Touching people inappropriately
No smiles - glum	No smiles - scowls
Irritating mannerisms	Irritating mannerisms - don't care
Stands in wrong place	Stands where he/she chooses
Moves around - sways	Moves around
Overdressed	Overdressed or scruffy
Hiding behind barriers (e.g. table)	Nodding "you will agree with me"

ASSERTIVE

lpful Behaviour Verbal - what we should say

all"

ɔs focus on key points and clear objectives, but is flexible

d scene setting and introductions

ɔerate repetitions and regular summaries

ıour

ıonal stories, examples and anecdotes

ɔle words, phrases and sentences

ds that encourage participation - asks questions

pical and well briefed

ıs the material

ses achievements of others

ɔurages questions from the audience

lpful Behaviour Vocal - how we should speak

s long pauses — Power Pauses

trols pace - usually slower than normal

ɔhasises

natically

dly

ırly with good enunciation

unduly concerned about accent

lpful Behaviour Visual - how we should look

ɛs significant eye contact to all - 2-3 seconds

les and shows emotion

orms

k Power Presence - the centre of attention

s bold gestures

ls with disruptions and distractions

ps to time

s interesting aids

ɔt dominated by PowerPoint

ks composed

ɛs to be different - takes well-prepared risks

What about Nerves?

When stressed our bodies want to fight or take flight.

Human Reactions	Likely Results	Implications
Thyroid hormon released into the bloodstream.	The shakes. Insomnia.	Take relaxation seriously.
Release of endorphin increased.	Natural pain killer released into body.	You will feel good when it s over.
Reduction in testosterone and progesterone.	Decreased sex drive.	It depends.
Shutdown of digestive system.	Rectum and bladder empty. Dry mouth and throat.	Go to toilet. Have water handy.
Release of sugar into bloodstream.	Aggravates diabetes.	No need for boost sugar levels.
Blood pumps faster.	Increased temperature. Sweating.	You will be the hott person in the room Plenty of deodoran
Increased air supply.	Breathing becomes faster.	Take slow deep breaths before you speak.
Concentration increases.	You can think more clearly.	Your notes can be BRIEF.
Pupils dilate.	Better all round vision.	Easier to make eye contact.
Hair stands up to make us appear bigger.	Unwanted hairs stand out.	Check in mirror.
Pigmentation changes.	Blotches and blushes.	Consider make up. Wear green if you blush.

PowerPoint

ot to be confused with Power Presence ( ) or the PowerPause)

reasons for using lots and lots and lots of PowerPoint...

1. Bill Gates is not rich enough
2. When you are creating your slides your colleagues will think you are doing something useful
3. You won't have to look at the audience
4. You think that sound and animation are trendy
5. The chief executive uses it
6. It gives you something to do with your hands
7. You want to obscure your message
8. You think it is good for your audience to have the chance to daydream
9. You can pretend to be invisible
10. A voice in your head says "PowerPoint is your master - you must obey..."

easons for using some PowerPoint

1. Graphical displays of data
2. For an interactive exercise
3. To reinforce amounts/quantities
4. To show pictures, photos
5. To display a quotation

oid slides showing bullet points and text, and remember t the B Key will Blank your screen when in slideshow w!

ave often regretted my speech, never my silence" - ymous.

The 3 Vs

When a listener is unsure of meaning, messages are received

VERBALLY	**7%**
VOCALLY	**38%**
VISUALLY	**55%**

Things to remember

Verbal Keep it Simple Stupid!
Never denigrate people or competitors.
Avoid 'Ums' and other irritating, useless words.
Think about using stories, examples, humour.

Vocal Speak slowly and loudly.
Be varied and dramatic.
Your 'everyday' voice is not your presenting voice.
The pause is a fantastic help.

Visual You are the number one visual!
Use your face to support your feelings. Smile more than us
Use bold gestures.
Avoid fidgets - move only for a purpose.
Give each person 2 - 3 seconds eye contact.

"No one really listens to anyone else, and if you try for a while you'll see why"
- Mignon McLaughlin.

Love Your Pause:

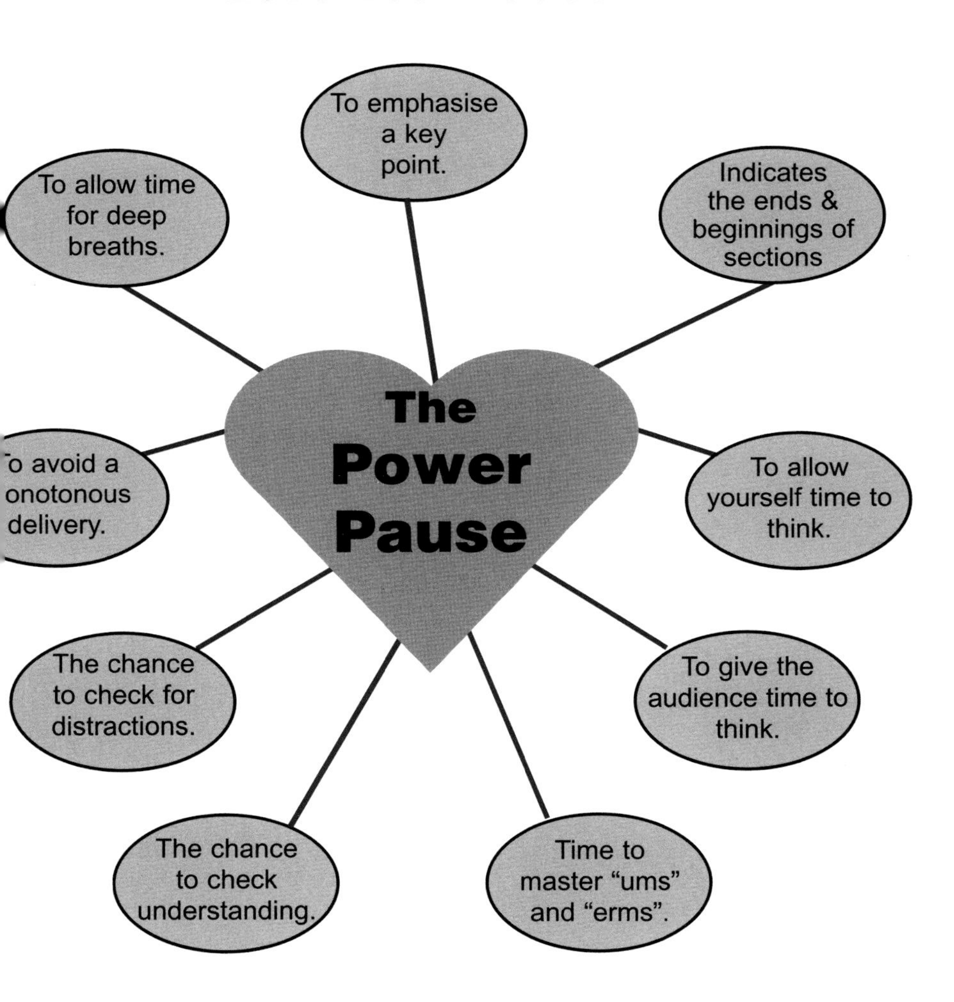

ave noticed that nothing I have never said ever did any harm"

vin Coolidge.

Question Time

"For you information let me ask you a question"
- Marshall McLahan

Question types	How to answer
SIMPLE	Grab the chance to be clear and concise.
OBSCURE/ MUDDLED	Ask the questioner to repeat, this will give time to think.
RHETORICAL	You do not have to answer unless you are questioned directly and clearly. Phrase a question yourself if you want.
ANTAGONISTIC	Stay calm, be brief, move on.
CLEAR/OPEN	Elaborate only if the audience look interes
UNANSWERABLE	Never guess. Say "I don't know but will fin for you".
MULTIPLE	Deal briefly with one at a time and ask the questioner what the other parts are as you finish each part.

"The less men think, the more they talk"
- Montesquieu.

\udience's expectations of the speaker.

NOWLEDGEABLE

but not a show off

ONEST

prepared to say "I don't know..."

STENER

doesn't jump in with answer

checks understanding of questioner to answer given

PROACHABLE

open gestures to all

friendly expressions and good eye contact

NTROLLING

allowing all to participate

encouraging the timid

discouraging the loudmouths

keeping track of time

keeping track of content

giving concise answers

URTEOUS

never sarcastic

answers to ALL the audience

smiles and entertains... the performance continues!

ealing with hostile questions:

Say if you cannot answer

Encourage help from the audience:

- Give them eye contact
- Gesture for their views/participation
- Turn your body away from the hostile questioner
- Be alert for a 'rescuing' question from an ally.
- Offer to deal with the issue later.

When Answering Questions

Your eye contact must go to **ALL** when you answer.

You are still performing !

Put away your prompts. Stay in control of the room. Use your PowerPresence. (☆)

Remember to stay in control of the pace of your voice. Pause when necessary.

Use gestures to reinforce your words and emotions.
Stand still.

Famous Speeches

passions are the only orators which always persuade."
ncois de La Rochefoucauld

Inaugural address January 20th, 1961
so, my fellow Americans: ask not what your country can do for you - ask you can do for your country.
ellow citizens of the world: ask not what America will do for you, but what her we can do for the freedom of man.

chill - June 18th, 1940
t General Weygand called the Battle of France is over. I expect that the e of Britain is about to begin. Upon this battle depends the survival of stian civilization. Upon it depends our own British life, and the long continuity ur institutions and our Empire. The whole fury and might of the enemy must soon be turned on us.
knows that he will have to break us in this Island or lose the war. If we can d up to him, all Europe may be free and the life of the world may move ard into broad, sunlit uplands. But if we fail, then the whole world, including Inited States, including all that we have known and cared for, will sink into byss of a new Dark Age made more sinister, and perhaps more protracted, e lights of perverted science.
s therefore brace ourselves to our duties, and so bear ourselves that if the h Empire and its Commonwealth last for a thousand years, men will still 'This was their finest hour'.

ham Lincoln – Gettysburg Address Nov 19 1863
score and seven years ago our fathers brought forth on this continent, a nation, conceived in Liberty, and dedicated to the proposition that all men reated equal.
we are engaged in a great civil war, testing whether that nation, or any n so conceived and so dedicated, can long endure. We are met on a great e-field of that war. We have come to dedicate a portion of that field, as a resting place for those who here gave their lives that that nation might live. It ogether fitting and proper that we should do this.
in a larger sense, we cannot dedicate -- we cannot consecrate -- we cannot w -- this ground. The brave men, living and dead, who struggled here, have ecrated it, far above our poor power to add or detract. The world will little nor long remember what we say here, but it can never forget what they did It is for us the living, rather, to be dedicated here to the unfinished work

that they who fought here have thus far so nobly advanced. It is rather for u be here dedicated to the great task remaining before us -- that from these honoured dead we take increased devotion to that cause for which they ga last full measure of devotion -- that we here highly resolve that these dead not have died in vain -- that this nation, under God, shall have a new birth c freedom -- and that government of the people, by the people, for the people shall not perish from the earth.

Martin Luther King - August 28th, 1963

So I say to you, my friends, that even though we must face the difficulties o today and tomorrow, I still have a dream. It is a dream deeply rooted in the American dream that one day this nation will rise up and live out the true meaning of its creed - we hold these truths to be self-evident, that all men a created equal.

I have a dream that one day on the red hills of Georgia, sons of former slav and sons of former slave-owners will be able to sit down together at the tab brotherhood.

I have a dream that one day, even the state of Mississippi, a state swelterir with the heat of injustice, sweltering with the heat of oppression, will be transformed into an oasis of freedom and justice.

I have a dream my four little children will one day live in a nation where the not be judged by the colour of their skin but by the content of their characte

I have a dream today!

I have a dream that one day every valley shall be exalted, every hill and mountain shall be made low, the rough places shall be made plain, and the crooked places shall be made straight and the glory of the Lord will be reve and all flesh shall see it together.

Beatitudes from the Sermon on the Mount by Jesus

Blessed *are the poor in spirit, for theirs is the kingdom of heaven.*

Blessed *are those who mourn, for they shall be comforted.*

Blessed *are the gentle, for they shall inherit the earth.*

Blessed *are those who hunger and thirst for righteousness, or they shall be satisfied.*

Blessed *are the merciful, for they shall receive mercy.*

Blessed *are the pure in heart, for they shall see God.*

Blessed *are the peacemakers, for they shall be called sons of God.*

Blessed *are those who have been persecuted for the sake of righteousnes for theirs is the kingdom of heaven.*

Blessed *are you when people insult you and persecute you, and falsely sa kinds of evil against you because of Me.*

King Henry V

Once more unto the breach,
dear friends, once more;
Or close the wall up with our English dead.
In peace there's nothing so becomes a man
As modest stillness and humility:
But when the blast of war blows in our ears,
Then imitate the action of the tiger;
Stiffen the sinews, summon up the blood,
Disguise fair nature with hard-favour'd rage;
Then lend the eye a terrible aspect;
Let it pry through the portage of the head
Like the brass cannon; let the brow o'erwhelm it
As fearfully as doth a galled rock
O'erhang and jutty his confounded base,
Swill'd with the wild and wasteful ocean.
Now set the teeth and stretch the nostril wide,
Hold hard the breath and bend up every spirit
To his full height. On, on, you noblest English.
Whose blood is fet from fathers of war-proof!
Fathers that, like so many Alexanders,
Have in these parts from morn till even fought
And sheathed their swords for lack of argument:
Dishonour not your mothers; now attest
That those whom you call'd fathers did beget you.
Be copy now to men of grosser blood,
And teach them how to war. And you, good yeoman,
Whose limbs were made in England, show us here
The mettle of your pasture; let us swear
That you are worth your breeding; which I doubt not;
For there is none of you so mean and base,
That hath not noble lustre in your eyes.
I see you stand like greyhounds in the slips,
Straining upon the start. The game's afoot;
Follow your spirit, and upon this charge
Cry 'God for Harry, England, and Saint George!'

Quotes by Winston Churchill

This report, by its very length, defends itself against the risk of being read.

A fanatic is one who can't change his mind and won't change the subject.

An empty taxi arrived at 10 Downing Street, and when the door was opened Atlee got out.

Ending a sentence with a preposition is something up with which we will not

Golf is a game who's aim it is to hit a very small ball into an even smaller ho with weapons singularly ill-designed for the purpose.

However beautiful the strategy, you should occasionally look at the results.

I am always ready to learn although I do not always like being taught.

I like pigs. Dogs look up to us. Cats look down on us. Pigs treat us as equal

I'm just preparing my impromptu remarks.

Success is going from failure to failure without losing your enthusiasm.

Broadly speaking, the short words are the best, and the old words best of al

NANCY ASTOR to Churchill:
If you were my husband I would put poison in your coffee.
CHURCHILL: *And if I were your husband, I would drink it.*

BESSIE BRADDOCK: *Mr Churchill, you are drunk.*
CHURCHILL: *And you madam, are ugly. But I shall be sober tomorrow.*

GEORGE BERNARD SHAW *(Telegram inviting Churchill to opening night of Pygmalion): Am reserving two tickets for you for my premiere. Come and bri friend - if you have one.*
CHURCHILL *wired back: Impossible to be present for the first performance. attend the second - if there is one.*

If you have an important point to make, don't try to be subtle or clever. Use pile driver. Hit the point once. Then come back and hit it again. Then hit it a time - a tremendous whack. Don't be nervous. Do just as I do. Whenever I g up to speak, I always make a point of taking a good look around the audienc Then I say to myself, 'What a lot of silly fools.' And then I always feel better. does not recommend this approach)

Team Briefing

anisational essentials for team briefing:

licy Document.

ership by senior management.

e - management structure.

mation at corporate level.

mation at local level.

o-way system.

ulti-channel option.

onitoring / evaluation system.

n briefing must be:

to Face - encouraging questions and ensuring understanding.

ams - between 4 - 15 people is recommended.

he Team Leaders - it is their responsibility to brief their own e.

ular - at least once a month for 30 minutes with dates set well in nce.

vant - the leader of the team providing information on Progress, le, Policy and Points for Action.

itored - by managers walking their place of work, asking questions itting in on briefings.

Plan well in advance:

Analyse your audience.

Avoid barriers by arranging a convenient, comfortable and quiet location.

Set up the room to encourage participation.

Arrange refreshments.

Consider a time suitable for all.

Decide on what resources you may need from props, flip chart, slides to g

speakers.

Prepare rough timings for delivering your material.

Become familiar with your material and decide on ways to bring it to life.

Research the answers to likely questions.

Deliver with a performance:

Begin by making a good first impression.

Remember that you are Number One.

Give strong eye contact and SMILE.

Show composure and courtesy.

Use relevant and understandable examples.

Always finish on a positive note.

Be in control at all times.

"A speech is like a love affair. Any fool can start it to end it requires considerable skill"
- Lord Mancroft

Planning the Brief

·oduction:

PACT. Begin by raising expectations. (*e.g. humour, a prop, a story, a quiz or similar ·ker*).

EED. Remind the audience why they need to listen. Mention a coming ·ght and remind them that their views are valued.

ME. Explain the timetable (and stick to it).

·SPONSE. Encourage the team to question you at any time.

UTLINE the AGENDA. Explain what is going to be covered.

·in items:

·ORATE: Select messages from recent communications that are relevant ·resting to your team. Exceptionally, you may need to convey messages to ·e that all staff receive the message at the same time in the same way.

RTMENTAL: Pass on, and discuss, relevant Departmental information.

·L: The opportunity for ALL the Team to talk about activities, achievements ·oncerns. To agree action points for next meeting etc.

·nmary:

·'s repeat the key points - who is going to do what, by when.

·estions:

·ive briefings are **TWO-WAY**.

·e manager s responsibility to encourage downwards, inter-divisional and ·d flows of information.

·e manager s responsibility to seek answers to questions.

Briefing Planning Sheet

TOPICS - Key Points	TIME	ACTIONS - By Wh / by When
INTRO: ▪ ▪ ▪		
CORPORATE: ▪ ▪ ▪		
DEPARTMENTAL: ▪ ▪ ▪		
LOCAL - People / Achievements etc ▪ ▪ ▪ ▪		
SUMMARY: ▪ ▪ ▪		
QUESTIONS from Team (To be followed-up by next meeting or earlier):		

Training

nanager, you may well be asked to deliver or assist training sessions. Before tart to plan training, consider the need to develop a **SMART** objective for module or section.

objectives must be:

CIFIC:	Clearly defined and easily identifiable to the learner.
.SURABLE:	The outcome of the training must be able to be measured in performance or behaviour.
IEVABLE:	Often training is expected to do what is not possible. It is usually the first in a long process of learning.
EVANT:	There must be clear benefits to trainees. These should be outlined in the INTRO and reinforced later.
ED:	It is common to try to squeeze too much into an event and rush through points that may need considerable reflection.

When setting objectives for staff ensure
that they are ***SMART***

ıe novice teacher shows and tells incessantly:
: wise teacher listens, prods, challenges,
ɪ refuses to give the right answer"
u Tzu.

How People Learn

Kolb's learning cycle is a simple and effective approach to training.

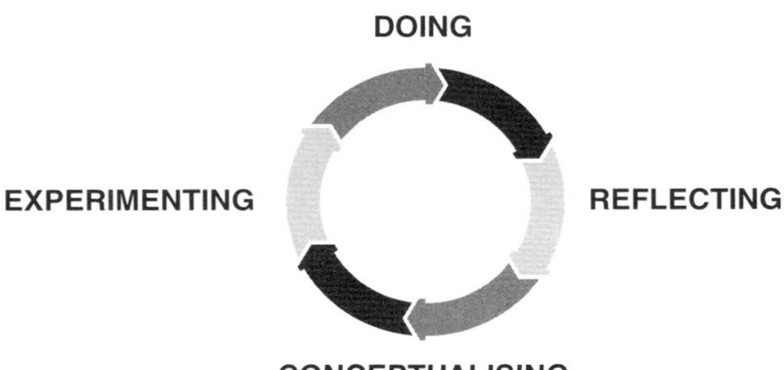

DOING: Gaining a worthwhile training experience in a realistic setting.

REFLECTING: Thinking about what you see and feel followin experience.

CONCEPTUALISING: Deciding whether and how the experiences wi valuable to you.

EXPERIMENTING: Trying things out within and outside the learnin environment.

Implications for the trainer:

The trainer should seek to incorporate varied methods (as per the cycle) i training event.

Post course support is essential-refresher courses should be considered.

Exercises that repeat the practice of the most important learning points essential.

Adequate time to think and encouragement to conceptualise must be includ the training design.

The training exercises should reflect real life as closely as possible.

Learning Styles

Adults have preferred learning styles.

ACTIVISTS

ve themselves freely

to enjoy new experiences

›pen minded and enthusiastic

rst then consider the
equences

e on new ideas, but may get
d later

to be active as often as
ible

REFLECTORS

Want to stand back and think

Collect data before acting

Tend to be cautious

Would naturally take a back seat in meetings etc

Enjoy observing others before acting

THEORISTS

: to base experiences on
›lished theory

‹ problems through in a step
ep way

to analyse

eciate theories, models,
mptions, systems etc

be uncomfortable with
ective judgements

PRAGMATISTS

Keen to try out new ideas and theories

Like to get things moving

Can become impatient with long explanations etc

Are practical and down to earth

'If it works, it's OK'

Reasons Why Learning May Not Take Place

No gain:

If the trainee sees that the training will not help their development, they ma
the necessary motivation to learn. The tutor must state the benefits explicit
and not assume that the trainees know what they are.

No personal responsibility for learning:

Through no fault of the tutor a trainee may not feel inclined or capable of ta
responsibility for the learning on offer.

Timeliness:

The training may be happening at a time when the trainee can not apply th
skills in the workplace.

Expectation:

If trainees have been programmed (perhaps by colleagues) to expect a
worthless, dull or complicated course, they will attend with the wrong attitu

Prior experience:

Trainees with poor previous experience of a type of training, or a certain tra
may attend with a closed mind.

Poor content:

Clearly a dull, poorly presented course will ensure the absence of learning

Poor control:

It is essential that the tutor maintains a firm grip on the mechanics of the tr
- him/her self, the environment, timing content, and audience.

Designing Exercises

Innovative and entertaining exercises are essential for excellent training courses

ıen designing exercises:

ys have a clear purpose in mind. What is it designed to achieve?

re that it delivers a successful outcome - start with simple activities and up complexity

it achievable and worthwhile

ıarse the duration e.g. before and during pilot courses

ɔnsistent with fonts, layout, terminology etc

.S. (Keep it simple, stupid).

ıen giving instructions:

re understanding by all

ly state the duration

adequate space and resources

the chance for questions

k during exercises that people have understood

t be tempted to give too much help too early

completion:

urage participants to speak to discover their progress, and the implications e exercise

ect errors

pare the experience of the group with that of previous groups

constructive feedback and praise where merited

k the participants understanding of your points

urage personal action plans

ys evaluate the value of the exercise

Triggers

A 'trigger' is any device that allows you to keep on track and focussed on your key points.

Prompt cards:
Use colour and write only a few key words on a smallish card.

Props:
Anything can act as a prop and the prop can be used to generate discussions, ideas and actions.

Exercises:
Items associated with exercises, e.g. sheets of paper, notebooks, etc will help you to remember what is to be done next.

Flip charts:
Pre-prepared flip charts, or small pencil written notes in the corner of a chart will help your continuity.

Questions:
Having pre-planned questions for the group will raise certain topics at an appropriate time.

Time:
You may decide that at a particular time of the day a certain exercise needs to begin to ensure that you meet your objectives.

Colleague:
A colleague may be programmed to intervene at a certain time to raise an issue or take over for a while.

Slides:
The appearance of a particular slide can introduce or conclude a part of the course. (Warning: Use powerPoint wisely)

Course Design

Course Title	
ience:	Aim and Objectives:
ation:	Delivery Method:

Day 1

odule	Timing	Topics	Objective
troduction	**9.00 - 9.30**	INTRO	To welcome trainees & prepare them for the event.
	10.30 -10.45		BREAK
	12.30 -13.30		LUNCH
	14.45 -15.00		BREAK
Review	**16.15 - 16.30**	Review What is to come	To reiterate & reinforce the key lessons of the day.
	16.30		CLOSE

Module Design

Course Title: **Time:**

Module:

Objective:

Topic	Key Points	Suppor
Intro	▪ ▪ ▪ ▪	
SUMMARY		

The Eternal Triangle

Responsibility for successful training lies with:

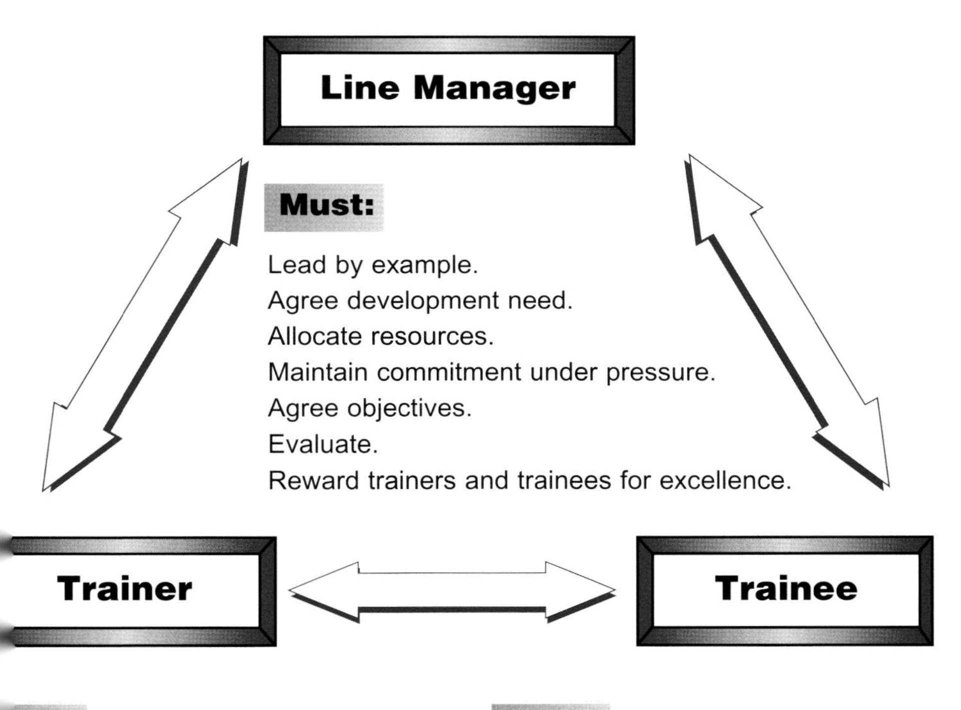

ust:

ee smart objectives.
lexible.
vide interactive, stimulating
ning opportunities.
trol the group.
uate.

Must:

Be open about needs.
Take responsibility for their learning.
Give considered feedback.
Value their opportunities to learn.

**e test of a preacher is that his congregation goes
y saying, not "What a lovely sermon" but, "I will do
ething!"**
Francis de Sales.

Training Essentials

GAIN ATTENTION **BE RELEVANT**
IMPROVE CONFIDENCE **PROVIDE SATISFACTION**

1 It is your duty to create an informal, non-threatening environment.

2 Develop an atmosphere of need - explain the benefits of learning.

3 Cater for different individual learning styles e.g. mix theory with exercises with reflection with facts - try to give something for everyone.

4 Acknowledge and value previous knowledge / experiences of individuals in the group.

5 Ensure that roles and responsibilities of the trainer and trainee are clearly outlined i.e. "I shall...", "in return...", "You will...".

6 Ensure a balance between mental and physical involvement.

7 Allow sufficient time for assimilation of messages and procedures.

8 Focus on the possible. Keep it Simple Stupid !

9 Measure the outcomes and be prepared to change.

10 You can t win em all - don t be put off by those with closed minds and grudges against the organisation.

"Remember, behaviour breeds behaviour".

"Politics is perhaps the only profession for which nc preparation is thought necessary"
- Robert Louis Stevenson

Motivation

Development

Coaching

Feedback

Stress

Change

Meetings

Motivation

Social psychologist Frederick Hertzberg proposes in his study, *Work an the Nature of Man*, **SATISFIERS** and **MOTIVATORS** as the determining factors of people's job performance.
SATISFIERS, concern the working conditions and environment, the wages, the benefits, and the degree of job security
MOTIVATORS comprise challenging and creative tasks, recognition b peers and seniors, personal responsibility, possibilities for promotion, a the subjective feeling of forming part of corporate culture.

Consider the dangers of ignoring the Motivators when dealing with your staff. What are the implications for you in getting the best out of your job and getting the best out of your work colleagues?

"Management means helping people to get the best out of themselves, not organising things."
- Lauren Appley

"Fantastic things happen - to the way we feel, to the way we make other people feel. All this simply by using positive words."
- Professor Leo F Buscaglia

"People ask the difference between a leader and a boss.... The leader works in the open, and the boss in covert. The leader leads and the boss drives."
- Theodore Roosevelt

"It is amazing what you can accomplish if you do not care who gets the credit."
- President Harry S Truman

"I praise loudly. I blame softly." - Catherine the Great

"I wouldn't say I was the best manager in the business. But I was in the top one." - Brian Clough

The Role of Managers in Successful Organisations

Managers set clear objectives and enable their staff to achieve them

Managers do not give orders - they regard themselves as facilitators, or servants who help others to succeed

Managers encourage initiative and those who question the established way of doing things

Managers give regular feedback

Managers hold regular meetings encourage questions and participation by all

Managers encourage staff to make their own decisions about how they achieve their objectives

Managers may help the achievement of day-to-day activities, but their presence is not essential

No-one is allowed to supervise or manage unless they have excellent communication skills with individuals and groups

od leaders must first become good servants"
ert Greenleaf.

The Manager's Role as a Staff Develope

Stage 1: Help to identify needs

Needs may arise through:

- Change of role
- Observation of poor performance
- Introduction of a new system
- New equipment
- Legislation
- Request by staff member

Stage 2: Plan the Response

Following the identification the manager should consider:

- Priorities
- Budgets
- Materials
- Fit with business plans
- Cover
- Availability

Learning options may include:

- Courses internal / external
- Computer based learning
- Conferences
- Projects
- Mentoring
- Coaching by supervisor / exper
- Books / Tapes
- Secondments
- Academic course
- Intranet / Internet

Stage 3: Implementation

Make sure the objectives are clear and how the learning will help the individu
Help with funding / release / cover
Ensure attendance at the learning event
Book time for review
Consider how new skills can be practiced
Offer continuing support and encouragement

Stage 4: Evaluation

Discuss outcome with staff member
Has the need been met?
What is next development stage for the learner?
Give opportunities for use
Evaluate the methods used and the providers
Consider if other people need this learning
Was it value for money?

I Grow - The 3E Staff Development Process

<table>
<tr><td colspan="2">ɔmpose self / Arrange the Room
ɔns
trol your behaviour / Avoid all distractions and barriers</td></tr>
<tr><td colspan="2">ıtroduction
ɔns
ɔome and relax - agree time - explain why session is required - note
ıg policy - request interaction</td></tr>
<tr><td>ioal
ly Questions
ck understanding of need?
long has it been necessary?
identified?
specific is requirement?
realistic?</td><td>Notes</td></tr>
<tr><td>easons
ly questions
evelopment necessary?
cost effective?
will it improve performance?
ımarise</td><td></td></tr>
<tr><td>ptions
ly questions
could development happen
ning, academic, shadowing,
, reading, internet, a project,
swap etc?
ıt are likely resource
ications for favoured option?
ımarise</td><td></td></tr>
<tr><td>/rap-up
ly questions
ıt is to be done?
en and by whom?
en / how evaluated?
ain manager s role
e a SMART Objective

ımarise</td><td></td></tr>
</table>

Giving Feedback

- Before you begin, consider if it will help the receiver
- Agree ground rules in advance
- Offer feedback on what you have seen not what others may have tol you
- Relate feedback to specific items of behaviour, not general impressio
- Describe what you see rather than judge it
- Focus on the achievable - that which can be changed
- Prioritise - Keep it simple
- Empower the interviewee - ask questions rather than make statemen
- Give specific praise as well as areas for improvement, but separate t positive from the negative. If you don t it will all sound negative
- Consider personal limits - continually monitor the impact of your comments

"When people talk, listen completely. Most people never listen"
- Ernest Hemingway.

Active Listening

I face-to-face communications listening should be active rather passive:

rriers to Active Listening:

:tivity:

ave a tendency to only listen to the things we wish to hear. We may entrate on what **we** think important not what is important to the speaker.

ng Speed / Thinking Speed:

use we think four times faster than we speak, we can easily jump ahead of is being said and, consequently, be distracted and start to have one of the 12,367 thoughts which occupy our minds during a normal day.

tions to the Speaker:

t you are sounds so loudly in my ear, that I can t hear what you say . sionally because of our prejudices we ascribe characteristics to a speaker nich we have no grounds and we give more or less weight to their nation than we should.

actions:

ny communication event to be effective, great attention must be paid to nating distractions caused by noise, light, temperature and people.

rative statements:

I displaying prejudices or views that may alienate your audience. n and over-use of anecdotes may have a negative effect.

e trouble with her is that she lacks the power of versation but not the power of speech"

rge Bernard Shaw.

Requirements of Active Listening:

Physical

It is necessary to indicate to people that you are listening. Therefore:

Face the speaker squarely.
Give good eye contact, though not a stare.
Show facial expressions that say "I am listening".
Have a controlled posture with no fidgets from hands or feet.
Do not cross arms or legs.
Use nods, smiles, gestures, raised eyebrows etc as appropriate.

Psychological

Just as your non-verbal behaviour is of the utmost importance it is essential you monitor and react to the non-verbal behaviour of the other participants. where there is any doubt the message will be delivered **vocally and visu**

Verbal

However, there are a number of things that can be done verbally to improve listening process and improve understanding:

Asking Questions: a positive way of showing the speaker that you are re listening. This allows you the chance to investigate and probe. It allows the speaker the chance to restate their case. **Summary** questions are particula valuable, as they indicate to the speaker that you have been listening.
e.g. "from what you have said, i understand..."

Giving encouragement: use supportive statements and noises to accompany your nods.
e.g. "Hmm", "Ah", "I see..." "That's interesting..."

Key Word Repetition: Picking out the most important words to encourag the speaker to say more.

Empathy: Indicating to the speaker that you are gathering the emotional context to show the speaker that you are in touch with their point of view.
e.g. "So you feel that..." or "It seems to you...".

Specification: Asking the speaker to be precise in the way he/she presen their opinions.***e.g. "On what occasions do you think you've been ignored?"***

g appropriate language: Consider the best way to phrase statements
uence the behaviour of others.
ction the value or otherwise of the following types of statement:

	Positive response (%)	Negative response (%)
osing Statements ***"I think the solution..."*** s a less valuable method ining agreement than...	**25**	**39**
gesting Statements: ***"Perhaps we could try to..."*** times out of ten, a suggestion owed by agreement.	**42**	**18**
ding Statements ***"That is important, how would it work if..."*** ing is often the best way in wholehearted support.	**32**	**11**

n people **disagree**, seven times out of ten, the disagreement will continue,
eas when people **agree**, eight times out of ten the other person will be
uraged to say more.

n a speaker asks for **clarification**, nine times out of ten it will be given.

valuable to appreciate how words and the way they are spoken influence
esponse of others and that the following types of statement will usually be
conducive to an open discussion than other types:

Clarifying	**Building**
Informing	**Suggesting**

**e world is dying for want, not of good preaching,
of good hearing"**
odrow Wilson

Ten Tip Top Time Management Tips

To improve your time management, commit yourself to **make drastic chang** Be creative to find and introduce different ways of working.

1. **Plan your working day/week and then protect the planned time.** This involve re-conditioning your environment, and the expectations of others. Yo are efficient the day before you start your holiday. Make every day like this.

2. **Check messages at planned times,** and avoid continuous notification o incoming emails. Restrict the time that you are free to take unplanned calls.

3. Arrange some **time-slots when you are not available. Plan preparatio and creative thinking time in your diary** for the long-term jobs - the short-t urgent tasks can use up all your time.

4. **Challenge your tendency to say 'yes'** - start asking and probing what is involved. Re-condition the expectations of others as to your availability.
Be assertive and prepared to say 'no'. Explain clearly why you are manag your time in this way and people will respect you for it.

5. Think about how you spend your time. If you don t know, **keep a time log**

6. Challenge anything and anyone that could be wasting time; particularly habitual tasks, meetings, reports etc. **Don't be a slave to a daft process or system.**

7. **Plan time slots for unplanned activities** - you may not know exactly wh you ll need to do, but if you plan the time to do it, then other important things not get pushed out of the way when the need arises.

8. When you have lots to do, make a list of what needs to be done and whe After this **handle each piece of paper only once.** Do one job at a time. Bre big tasks down into stages and plan time-slots for them.

9. Keep a **clean desk and well-organized systems.** Review your work environment, layout, IT equipment, etc, so they can be used efficiently.

10. **Delegate** when appropriate.

Why Delegation is Important

od delegation can bring many benefits

e time to manage
able development for staff
eans of motivating staff
e job satisfaction
ater sense of responsibility for staff
d working environment
e staff involvement
e respect from staff
roved teamwork

y managers don't delegate

umed lack of competence of subordinates
ception that It is quicker to do it myself . Maybe, in the short term
manager enjoys the task
manager has always done it
uctant to share knowledge - knowledge is power
- wishes to appear a martyr
r - that the person who takes on the task may do it better than the
manager
r protective of staff - not wishing to appear to overload
tics - top management would not approve
k of delegation skills
knowing what to delegate
ing no one to delegate to

the last three in this list are genuine reasons not to delegate, and all but the an be overcome by improving your skills.

e surest way for an executive to kill himself is to se to learn how, when and to whom to delegate k" - J.C. Penny.

Delegation

Five steps for Effective Delegation

Clarify the task and your expectations. Check understanding. Make notes if necessary.

Enthusiastically explain limits of authority, the availability of resources, and the timescales.

Set aside time for regular but informal discussions on progress. Deal with the big picture, not details.

Allow the delegate to have as much freedom as possible, but monitor progress, and be available.

Evaluate the outcome. Praise success - learn from mistakes. **The manager is ultimately responsible.**

Meetings MISERY

hy meetings become miserable:

1 Drifting off the topic

2 Lack of leadership

3 No natural daylight - poor environment

4 Meetings for meeting s sake

5 The broken record
(someone making the same point over and over and over again)

6 Running over time

7 Meetings with no purpose

8 Interruptions from mobiles and messages

9 Refreshments not refreshed regularly

10 The cynic
(someone who criticises but rarely has constructive ideas)

11 People not taking them seriously

12 Poor preparation by key participants

"The greatest problem in communication is the illusion that it has been accomplished"- George Bernard Shaw

"Perhaps Hell is nothing more than an enormous conference of those who, with little or nothing to say, take an eternity to say it" - Dudley C. Stone

"A good sign that either the meeting or some of the people are superfluous is when they try to get out of coming" - Robert Heller

"Meetings are indispensable when you don't want to do anything" - J K Galbraith

Participating in Meetings

Preparation

Be up to date with minutes, agendas - every document that has relevance to the meeting.

Make notes of the key issues you wish to raise or have been asked to report on.

Consider your body language, your timing, and with what verbal and vocal control you will ask questions.

Dress up for the occasion, look and feel impressive.

Consider the reaction of the audience to your interventions - try to win before you speak by gaining some key allies to a contentious point.

Structure:

Tell the chair in advance what you wish to raise.

Have a beginning, middle and an end, just like a presentation.

Don t waffle. Get to the point quickly and be explicit, accurate and precise.

Control:

Stay calm and purposeful; don t rise to the bad manners or loss of control by others.

Evaluate how the meeting is going to consider amending your style and content - be flexible.

Listen effectively to the contributions of others - use eye contact, nods and smiles as appropriate.

Practice:

Don t worry if you do not achieve all your goals every time - be prepared to lose, but return with increased determination.

Chairing Meetings

paration

'ourself, Is the meeting necessary ?

the right people been invited? - small groups will often reach ions more quickly. Anticipate their needs and agendas .

e early, check beforehand that the room is appropriate and has the relevant ies.

all relevant documents, have a clear focus on your objectives.

luce people informally before the meeting and formally welcome new pers.

cture:

with an INTRO, show enthusiasm, remind them of the objectives, ong it will last and rules about questions and interruptions (i.e. through the).

narise each item and the action required.

trol:

ay active listening and always be positive.

lear rules about breaks, interruptions, messages, phones etc.

n the clock to share time appropriately - curtail those who waffle or date.

re all who want to speak are given the opportunity.

uestions to clarify not just for yourself but for those in the group night be uncertain.

ots of patience and humour - never put down participants. urage this in others.

ot get bogged down on detail, and be prepared to agree other s to make progress e.g. sub-groups, defer items, setting individual n points.

ctice:

uate your success regularly - seek advice and help from the ipants.

Assertive Behaviour in Meetings

Verbal / Vocal	Visual
Use simple unambiguous words	Use facial expression including smiles to encourage
Be concise, accurate and honest	Nod and gesture in agreement
Use stories, anecdotes and humour (but don t ramble on)	Be aware that your face and particularly you eyes are betraying emotions
Stick to the subject	Give friendly and expressive eye contact
Ask the chair politely to move on or spend more time on an issue if he / she is losing control	Bring and use visual aids and prop
Ask for clarification of points	Stand if necessary to make your points
Don t interrupt or be seen to be argumentative	Sit up straight or lean forward sligh to show extra enthusiasm

If you need to use aggressive or submissive behaviour (in an assertive, there controlled way) to make your point, do so sparingly.

By adopting the above, you will be regarded as a POWERFUL participant in meetings.

Managing Change

ange is inevitable and resistance is to be expected:

he Emotional Cycle of Change

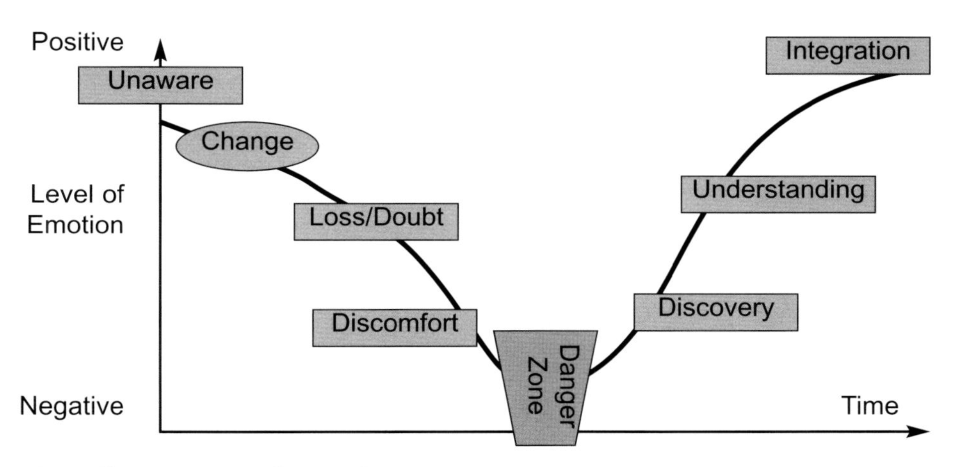

plan for managing change

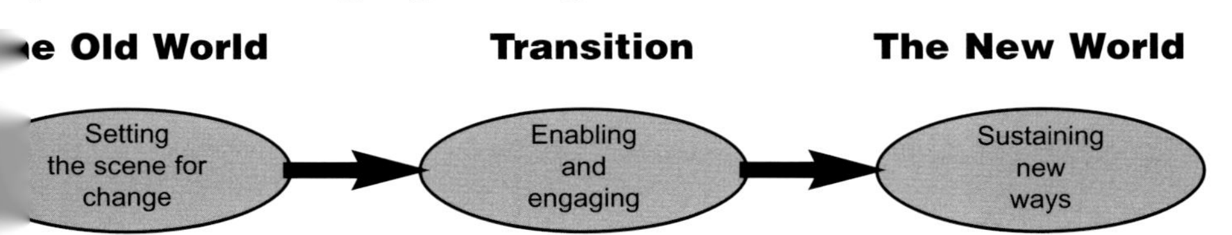

Old World - Set the scene for change — honour the past. If past practices not publicly valued, people spend time justifying the past and this hampers mitment to the future.

nsition - During the change, it is normal for feelings of disorientation to . Maintain momentum and continually reaffirm the goal. Change agement requires building and sharing the vision.

New World - Sustain new ways. Celebrate achievements and replace onal losses with personal gains. This is the time to draw a line in the sand.

Resistance to Change

Resistance	Cause	Approach
"I don t get it."	Lack of information.	Communicate. Use the language the other per will be comfortable witl and give examples
"I don t like it."	Emotional. Fear of inadequacy and/or loss of status.	Use effective communication and listening skills to explo the reasons
"I don t like you."	The message is coming from a source regarded as suspect by the recipient.	Facilitate. Begin by repairing burned bridge and building relationsh

Change management essentials

1. Communicate, Communicate, Communicate
2. Senior managers must own the change
3. Senior managers must communicate
4. The communication must be two-way and sometimes face-to-face
5. Those who resist should not be regarded as subversive
6. With IT implementations the views of user-groups should be acted upon
7. Training should be available to explain new processes and new systems
8. The training should be as simple as possible
9. Specialists/expert users should be enlisted, trained and supported

"The universe is change; our life is what our thoug make it."

— Marcus Aurelius Antonius

Stress

Possible Cause	Possible solution
verwork	Delegate Prioritise tasks and agree SMART objectives Engage more resources Reflect on time management ideas
derwork	Explain your aspirations to management Seek development opportunities Consider part-time educational opportunities Volunteer for new, more challenging tasks
dequate manager	Prioritise tasks and agree SMART objectives Change your job Use assertive behaviour to manage him/her Remember, your manager may be more stressed than you and looking for help
dequate staff	Do all you can to develop their skills Communicate your feelings and expectations Actively listen to their views Allocate more time to help them to change Set a good example
sive manager eers	Explain your boundaries Keep a log of incidents Remind yourself that bullying or harassment is unacceptable Seek help from colleagues / staff representatives
sonal Problems	Your colleagues are usually very keen to help Talk to your manager to see how your work responsibilities may be amended Ensure staff use their holiday entitlement

ess is not what happens to us. It's our response to t happens. And RESPONSE is something we can ose." - Maureen Killoran

Preventing Job Stress in Staff

Action Points for Managers

Be on the alert for tell-tale signs of stress and the likely causes

Ensure that the workload is in line with each staff member s capabilities and resources

Design jobs to provide meaning, stimulation, and opportunities for staff

Clearly define roles and responsibilities — give SMART objectives

Give staff opportunities to participate in decisions and actions affecting their jc

Use Team meetings and coaching sessions to improve access to new skills, reduce uncertainty about career development, and future employm prospects

Provide opportunities for social interaction among staff

Establish work schedules that are compatible with demands and responsibilit outside the job

Do not be defensive concerning feedback about self from staff

Encourage staff to act in the above ways towards the people who work for them

Ensure staff take their holiday entitlement

Lead by example and avoid setting an expectation of presenteeism

Let the ends justify the means, if the work can be done flexibly

Explore opportunities for celebration and fun, but don t make it compulsory

Always try to improve the working environment

"Don't tell my mother I'm in politics: she thinks I play the piano in a whorehouse." Mark Twain

ople on Top 2

Prior-Sheridan is the well-known Sorbonne educated, ving super-mum, darling of the gossip columnists, and chief tive of BlueStocking Personnel. She has won many gious business awards and regularly appears on late night ion as a pundit on contemporary living. Over the past three BlueStocking s turnover has increased by a remarkable 700%. as she done this? We phoned Polly and put to her these searching questions.

is your favourite colour?
My cars are all blue, darling.

are you wearing today?
silk bodice ruffle dress from Narciso Rodriguez, blue shoes from Jimmy Choo, and chiffon shawl made by peasants in Baluchistan.

do you juggle the demands of motherhood with those of a high-ered career?
dn't do it without my wonderful team. I have Suki who is in charge of the children; who deals with the day-to-day nitty-gritty of the business; then there's Hester my who's a treasure; Charles my personal trainer; and Mrs. Charlesworth and her team re in charge of keeping the houses and flats in good order. Oh…I nearly forgot s that very important man who keeps me on my toes, my butler, Franz.

do you keep your great figure?
hree miles per day and then spend an hour in the gym. I eat only organic ables from Madagascar. The rumours about my visits to Harley Street are almost ly untrue.

t is your favourite music?
Mitchell's "Blue", I also like anything by Blue.

name has been linked to that of several eligible men; have you hing to say about that?
nportant for the BlueStocking brand to be associated with glamour and excitement. I taken it upon myself to be seen in the company of those who are the icons of the This causes me to be present at all the prestigious events of the Season and in exotic locations. Although my rivals sneer at my lifestyle my one concern is to nise shareholder returns.

ou have any advice for aspiring entrepreneurs?
s look and feel your best, my dear. Men should spend that little bit extra to buy that e, whilst ladies should never buy perfume from supermarkets.

People on Top 3

Many may feel that our Lords of the Realm are products of a bye-gone age and should go back there, but you may be surprised at how influential members of the Upper House have become in the boardrooms of the twenty first century. Take the **Earl of Wesham-in-Medlar**, for example, he is chairman of a leading international energy company and sits on the board of six major multi-nationals. He is the Queen s Silver Rod in Waiting, Master of the Buckinghamshire Hunt and pa of the Royal Society for the Succour and Relief of Distressed Gentlefolk.

What is your favourite colour?
Er, I'm not really sure. No one's asked me that before. Fascinating!

What are you wearing?
Ermine – I'm due to speak in the House in ten minutes. I'm supporting a proposal to more wind farms and oil exploration in the Lake District. Essential!

Are Peers relevant in today's society?
I can't speak for some of these new boys, ex-Polytechnic lecturers, failed Union lead pop stars and other assorted rabble, but I do feel there is a place for people with bre and character who know a thing or two about the achievements of the Carthaginians Papua New Guinea Tribal customs, I can speak a bit of Hiri Motu you know. Damn u

Current Reading?
Don't have much time for that sort of thing but when I do I like to browse A.L. Hetherington's' The Early Ceramic Wares of China'. Entrancing!

Inexcusable Luxury?
A large part of Northumberland - Marvellous County! Oh and most of Dorset - charm place!

Is it what you know or who you know?
Definitely what you know. Some people may say that the fact that my Great Great G aunt was the King's mistress has been a factor in the subsequent successes of our family, but one can't just sit around living in the past, one must keep up to date and h one's skills. Why last week I had one of those new computer thingies installed in my office – it even lets me play Patience. Extraordinary! Yes, I am sure I have got to whe am today by knowing what makes people tick and where to get a decent lunch when Sultan of Brunei gives you a call. Have to toddle off now, jolly good!

ople on Top 4

les Higginbottom, founder of Higgy-Bot Solutions is an
ɔle of someone who has grasped the tentacles of the
ɔlogical revolution and built a multi-million pound empire
the last five years through the development of innovative
:ts that are a factor in all our everyday lives. We asked him
e rose from his humble beginnings in Rotherham to succeed in this fast moving

: do you have for breakfast?
*have time for breakfast. I'm either on my plane, at the airport or on my way to or
he airport.*

was your first hi-tech product?
*I was at school, at Heckythump Comprehensive, I repackaged Blu-tack and sold it
gical Moon Clay, brought to earth by astronauts. The mark up was 500%. I later
ified into Mars Water.*

: are you developing on at the moment?
*one moment in time I have several innovations on the go. For example, I am
ıg with boffins in Shanghai to produce a kettle that whistles a Beatles song of your
when it boils. I am also working with the Ministry of Defence on a hush-hush
t related to the identification of terrorist suspects through their emission of body
s and their choice of ringtones for their mobiles.*

ur home life affected by this demanding schedule?
*homes in Barbados, San Diego, Brisbane and Ascot, but my wife and children
e to live in Barnsley. I see them when I can.*

: are you reading?
*f my gadgets reads books to me as I sleep. It's amazing! It is currently reading me
ɔf the Rings – it's about naval warfare between Japan and Paraguay in fourteenth
y Switzerland – the dog's the real hero.*

what you know or who you know?
*chool at 16 with no qualifications; all I had was the ten thousand pounds I made on
ɔon Clay and the Mars Water. God or something, has given me the ability to enter
agination of ordinary people to be able to tell them what they really wanted before
new it themselves. If you feel you have that gift then go for it. You don't need
cations to get `on' all you need is nouse!*

Don't Get Fooled again!

Sometimes trainers may ask you to participate in spurious listening exercise like this one, and call it an "intelligence" test to humiliate you.

1. If you are in a race and you overtake the person in second place, in what position do you finish?

2. Some months have 30 days and some have 31. How many have 28?

3. How far can a dog run into the woods?

4. If a doctor gave you three pills and told you to take one every half hour, how long would they last?

5. If you have two coins totalling 11 pence and one of them is not a 10 pence piece, what are the two coins?

6. A house is built with four sides, each wall having a southern aspect. What colour is the bear that passes the house each day?

7. Divide 30 by a half and add ten.

8. How many animals of each species did Moses take into the Ark?

9. What was the Prime Minister s name in 1987?

10. If you drove a bus with 42 people in it from London, stopped at Watford pick up 7 more passengers and to drop off 5, then at Luton you picked u more passengers, finally arriving at Edinburgh twenty minutes late, what the name of the driver?

11. Is it legal for a man to marry his widow's sister?

Sometimes you may be asked to participate in a spurious reading exercise as the following — Count the number of times the letter F or f appears in the following statement:

Fifty fit fighting men from the frigate Formidable were the pride of the Fleetw branch of the Royal Marines on account of their fearsome faces.

(Answers on Page

"Make sure you have finished speaking before your audience has finished listening"
- Dorothy Sarnoff

rd words to spell

ck your ability to spell these commonly misspelt words:

Innoculate	Inoculate	Inocculate
Occurrence	Ocurrance	Ocurance
Irrisistable	Irresistible	Iresistible
Milenium	Millenium	Millennium
Supercede	Superceed	Supersede
Accidentally	Acidentally	Accidently
Minuscule	Miniscule	Minniscule
Acommodate	Accommodate	Accomodate
Desicate	Desiccate	Dessicate
Laison	Liaison	Liason
Harass	Harras	Harrass
Definitely	Definately	Definitley
Embarass	Enbarras	Embarrass
Cemetary	Cemetery	Cematary
Occasion	Occassion	Ocassion
Weird	Wierd	Weerd
Diarrhoea	Dierhea	Diarrhea
Ecxtasy	Ecstassy	Ecstasy

(Answers on page 108)

What famous songs teach us about wo

Hotel California (The Eagles) A warning about the perils of working in the hospitality indu
We are told of a hotel where the lobby is choked with people who have checked out but a
unable to leave. Consequently, they spend the day lounging on the chairs in reception, le
at the receptionists and smelling worse and worse as their personal hygiene deteriorates.

Last Christmas (Wham) Christmas flings seldom last longer than the pine needles on the
Christmas tree. This thoughtful song reminds us that after several glasses of plonk, even
from Accounts has an air of mystery and subdued excitement about him, but come the da
he is the boring old pedant he always was.

Brown Sugar (Rolling Stones) It is a well-known fact that it is little things, like someone s
annoying laugh, that can cause the most irritation at work. In this song we are reminded t
for some, coffee is just not the same with white sugar and that if someone uses their
personally labelled supply of brown, dire consequences can occur. To compound the felon
they would probably use a damp spoon!

Legs (ZZ Top) "She s got legs and she knows how to use em". Sexism often works for wo
who show off their legs in this way. They invariably get promoted and leave a trail of bitter
from men and other women with less attractive legs.

Still Haven't Found What I'm looking for (U2) Yes you may have a boat in the Medway and
caravan in Wales, but what have you sacrificed to achieve those things? Has it been wort
missing your son s nativity plays and your daughter s first violin concert? And what will yo
with fourteen bathrobes from assorted Hilton Hotels? Get a life!

Are You Lonesome Tonight /Heartbreak Hotel (Elvis Presley) Inspired by consultants who
spend much of their life away from friends and family in lonesome apartments or hotel roo
living off room service and watching films that they would never watch if they had a choice
Their only consolation is their unrivalled collection of bathrobes (see above).

When I'm 64 (The Beatles) Only one year to go before retirement and concern about
pensioner poverty pervades this song. Evil cyborg designers have most likely robbed the
company pension scheme to spend the money on narcotics, and worries abound about lo
food, and loss of hair. The only hope is to sponge off Vera Chuck and Dave when they gro
up.

Road to Nowhere (Talking Heads) This is almost certainly about trying to catch the 17.30
to New York only to find yourself stuck for several hours on the M25 watching as your plar
dips its wings to you as you watch it leave Heathrow.

My Way (Frank Sinatra) When you retire, don t get so self absorbed that you have to bore
everyone with your innermost thoughts about life and work. All you have to do is accept th
golf clubs gracefully, say thank you to everyone, especially Sandra, and the get stuck into
wine and the buffet. In other words, leave with dignity.

The E- Learning Cycle

1. New Personnel Director appointed

2. Personnel Director is concerned about the size of the Training Budget

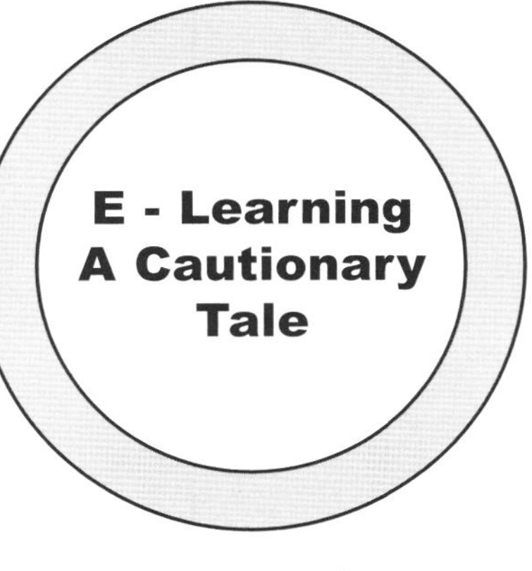

3. Reads article about the success of E-learning

4. Invites Mega E-Learning Inc to propose solution

5. Accepts $3.0 million tender from Mega E-Learning Inc

6. Implements E-Learning and closes Training Dept.

er 6 months
eople have
E-Learning
m

3. Personnel
Director resigns.

9. Training Dept reinstated

acts About E-Learning

omputing Magazine (9 December 2004) revealed that the UK s 'university for
ndustry' Ufi generated just £995,018 from businesses and individuals in 2003,
aving so far spent almost £1bn of public money.

n 2004 the NHS in the UK, cancelled a major E-Learning procurement project
esigned to support online training for many of the NHS's 1.2 million staff

he UK Government through the Higher Education Funding Council for England
as invested £62m in a University based E-Learning programme that was being
sed by only 140 students in June 2004. Dr Ian Gibson, who chairs the science
nd technology committee at the House of Commons, called the UK's e-university
an absolute disaster".

5 per cent of firms admitted that they have had their fingers burnt through using
-learning, according to a survey of 275 HR decision makers by e-learning
onsultancy ICUS.

The Way we used to work

Charles Dickens was one of the most accurate observers of charact Chapter Four of "Hard Times" a play set in Coketown (aka Preston), introduces readers to an entrepreneur and banker, Mr. Bounderby.

Why, Mr. Bounderby was as near being Mr. Gradgrind's bosom friend, as a man perfectly c of sentiment can approach that spiritual relationship towards another man perfectly devoid sentiment. So near was Mr. Bounderby - or, if the reader should prefer it, so far off.

He was a rich man: banker, merchant, manufacturer, and what not. A big, loud man, with a stare, and a metallic laugh. A man made out of a coarse material, which seemed to have b stretched to make so much of him. A man with a great puffed head and forehead, swelled in his temples, and such a strained skin to his face that it seemed to hold his eyes open, a his eyebrows up. A man with a pervading appearance on him of being inflated like a balloc and ready to start. A man who could never sufficiently vaunt himself a self-made man. A m who was always proclaiming, through that brassy speaking-trumpet of a voice of his, his ol ignorance and his old poverty. A man who was the Bully of humility.

A year or two younger than his eminently practical friend, Mr. Bounderby looked older; his or eight and forty might have had the seven or eight added to it again, without surprising anybody. He had not much hair. One might have fancied he had talked it off; and that what left, all standing up in disorder, was in that condition from being constantly blown about by windy boastfulness.

In the formal drawing-room of Stone Lodge, standing on the hearthrug, warming himself be the fire, Mr. Bounderby delivered some observations to Mrs. Gradgrind on the circumstanc its being his birthday. He stood before the fire, partly because it was a cool spring afternoo though the sun shone; partly because the shade of Stone Lodge was always haunted by th ghost of damp mortar; partly because he thus took up a commanding position, from which subdue Mrs. Gradgrind.

'I hadn't a shoe to my foot. As to a stocking, I didn't know such a thing by name. I passed t day in a ditch, and the night in a pigsty. That's the way I spent my tenth birthday. Not that a was new to me, for I was born in a ditch.'
Mrs. Gradgrind, a little, thin, white, pink-eyed bundle of shawls, of surpassing feebleness, mental and bodily; who was always taking physic without any effect, and who, whenever sh showed a symptom of coming to life, was invariably stunned by some weighty piece of fact tumbling on her; Mrs. Gradgrind hoped it was a dry ditch?

'No! As wet as a sop. A foot of water in it,' said Mr. Bounderby.

Enough to give a baby cold,' Mrs. Gradgrind considered.

'Cold? I was born with inflammation of the lungs, and of everything else, I believe, that was capable of inflammation,' returned Mr. Bounderby. 'For years, ma'am, I was one of the mos miserable little wretches ever seen. I was so sickly, that I was always moaning and groanin

ıs so ragged and dirty, that you wouldn't have touched me with a pair of tongs.'
s. Gradgrind faintly looked at the tongs, as the most appropriate thing her imbecility could ık of doing.

ɔw I fought through it, I don't know,' said Bounderby. 'I was determined, I suppose. I have ɘn a determined character in later life, and I suppose I was then. Here I am, Mrs. Gradgrind, ʌhow, and nobody to thank for my being here, but myself.'

ɜ. Gradgrind meekly and weakly hoped that his mother -

mother? Bolted, ma'am!' said Bounderby.

. Gradgrind, stunned as usual, collapsed and gave it up.

mother left me to my grandmother,' said Bounderby; 'and, according to the best of my ıembrance, my grandmother was the wickedest and the worst old woman that ever lived. If I a little pair of shoes by any chance, she would take 'em off and sell 'em for drink. Why, I e known that grandmother of mine lie in her bed and drink her four-teen glasses of liquor ɔre breakfast!'

Gradgrind, weakly smiling, and giving no other sign of vitality, looked (as she always did) an indifferently executed transparency of a small female figure, without enough light behind

kept a chandler's shop,' pursued Bounderby, 'and kept me in an egg-box. That was the cot y infancy; an old egg-box. As soon as I was big enough to run away, of course I ran away. ı I became a young vagabond; and instead of one old woman knocking me about and ʼing me, everybody of all ages knocked me about and starved me. They were right; they no business to do anything else. I was a nuisance, an incumbrance, and a pest. I know that well.'

ɔride in having at any time of his life achieved such a great social distinction as to be a ınce, an incumbrance, and a pest, was only to be satisfied by three sonorous repetitions of oast.

s to pull through it, I suppose, Mrs. Gradgrind. Whether I was to do it or not, ma'am, I did it. ɘd through it, though nobody threw me out a rope. Vagabond, errand-boy, vagabond, ırer, porter, clerk, chief manager, small partner, Josiah Bounderby of Coketown. Those are ntecedents, and the culmination. Josiah Bounderby of Coketown learnt his letters from the des of the shops, Mrs. Gradgrind, and was first able to tell the time upon a dial-plate, from ing the steeple clock of St. Giles's Church, London, under the direction of a drunken e, who was a convicted thief, and an incorrigible vagrant. Tell Josiah Bounderby of town, of your district schools and your model schools, and your training schools, and your kettle-of-fish of schools; and Josiah Bounderby of Coketown, tells you plainly, all right, all ct - he hadn't such advantages - but let us have hard-headed, solid-fisted people - the ıtion that made him won't do for everybody, he knows well - such and such his education however, and you may force him to swallow boiling fat, but you shall never force him to ess the facts of his life.'

But what was it like to be working for a character like Mr Bounderby?

We have obtained the previously unpublished diary of Harriet Earnshaw, an employee in the Thrift Mill, in Heckmondwyke, Yorkshire. After working half-days at the Mill, Harriet left school, 1900, at the age of twelve, to work there full-time as a Warp operative. Her diaries give a fascinating insight into management and work practices at the turn off the last century. Here we reproduce many of her entries that have echoes of the management challenges face today.

Motivation

Because the woollen mills of Yorkshire were busy and wages were steadily rising, manageme could not take it for granted that staff would stay in their posts. At Thrift Mill efforts were made reward hard working employees.

Tuesday 4 May 1903 *I confess that today was unusual. Because we completed an extremely large consignment of warp for our troops in Kwazululand, Mr Shawforth, the Senic OverWarper personally shook the hand of everyone in the Warp room. We didn't know what say so we all curtsied, as though we were meeting the King! Today I wore my bonnet with the cream band.*

Discipline

There was no little scope for organised labour in the Mill and the middle managers ruled with strict disciplinary code.

Thursday, October 14th 1904 *Betsy Ramsbotham was fined one penny today for havi dirty fingernail. Sarah Boothroyd was fined half penny for failing to smile enough on Lord Arkwright's birthday. I had a nasty cold but managed to smile whenever one of the Underlookers walked past. I bought a new ribbon for my favourite bonnet today and I shall attach it on Sunday.*

Leadership Styles

Almost all of the managers at the Thrift Mill were internally appointed and leadership training was limited to what people had picked up from their time in the forces.

Wednesday 21st October 1905 *As we arrived at work today Seth Thirlington, the Foreman Overwarper, lined us up and led us in a hearty rendition of 'Hearts of Oak' to celebrate the hundredth anniversary of the Battle of Trafalgar when Lord Nelson saved us f the cruel intentions of the French and Spanish. He then made a little speech saying how ha we should work in honour of the sacrifice of our jolly jack tars. Needless to say we produce vast amounts of warp that day. On my way home my bonnet blew off in the strong wind an dirty in a puddle!*

Team Briefing

From the moment the workers entered the Mill at 6.30 until they departed at 5.00 they were expected to work and work hard.

Tuesday 15th May 1902 *During our lunch break all the machines in the mill fell silent. the fettlers seemed to go quiet. Mr Throssel the Senior UnderWarper came in with a smile* e and called us all into a huddle. He stood on a bail of warp endings and announced that ·rible Boers had finally surrendered to our brave lads and consequently, Lord Arkwright e could have an extra five-minute lunch break. We all gave three hearty cheers and se Edith Arrowsmith's son, Frederick, was serving in South Africa we gave her three as well! I put a flower (a bluebell) in my bonnet that night to celebrate.*

rmance Appraisal

Thrift Mill there was no formal appraisal system and instant dismissal was often the first would know that their performance was not up to scratch.

esday 3rd November 1905 *Mr Throssel came up to me today and asked me my He said he thought I was doing "right well'. I was thrilled. He then said he had his eye on d that there might be a vacancy for a Junior Underwarper when Mrs Fothergilll retires to ter her husband who has gone daft. I heard that Clarence Cartwright who I thought was ourite for that job was told off for wearing his cap at a jaunty angle. I resolved to buy a onnet at the market on Friday evening.*

ing

a new machine was installed the workers had to stay behind to be given instruction in its ften new machines led to redundancies.

sday 25th February 1906 *I felt rather drowsy today because of the flu and was most ed to be kept back one hour to be shown the workings of the new Warping Engine. It is ly a fine piece of equipment and I was asked to thread some yarn into the six spindles d the new warping frame. I must admit I felt rather proud. Tomorrow we are to use the ngine. The heavy rain on the way home soaked my bonnet. I felt damp and miserable as I nis entry.*

ays

July, the Mill shut down for a "Wakes" week to allow their staff a hard earned rest and trip seaside. In this extract from her diary Harriet, describes the excitement of her day out to ambe.

ay, 8 July 1905. *We had a lie-in today and didn't leave for the station until 6.30. We d off in pairs; I walked with Sally Postlethwaite from the Teasel room. (we were a bit slow ount of Sally's rickets) I didn't say anything, but my bonnet was much nicer than hers. ation was thronging with people all in their Sunday best. Lord Arkwright left first in his train, and we happily followed singing away as our train chuffed to Morecambe - a al place I thought I would never see! The day was a blur of laughter and dancing, cups of d cream cakes – we hardly noticed the rain! In Happy Mount Park, Walter Grizenthwaite nior Wefting Underlooker gave me a smile! When we returned to Heckmondwyke at 9.00 ening, I couldn't stop smiling.*

ther extract from her diary, Harriet tells of the annual cricket match between a team from efters and Weavers and one from the Warpers and Treadlers.

ay, July 25th 1906. *After chapel, we trooped off, in pairs, to Arkwright Hall for the l cricket match. I wore my bonnet with the green band. Lord Arkwright captained the s and Weavers, and because of his unbeaten double century, they made 475 for 6. W.G. a brilliant 14! After lunch the Warpers and Treadlers made a disappointing 37. We were ated to a pint of beer and a buttered scone. I felt rather tipsy on my way home.*

1908 Harriet Earnshaw became Mrs Harriet Grizenthwaite.

Never travel without

A guide for the business traveller to London

Item	Uses
Earplugs	To avoid being awoken at 5.00 a.m. b the reversing rubbish cart
Set of Spanners	To fix the combination bath / shower to enable you to choose the way you wash
Bottle of wine	To avoid the temptation of the mini ba and awkward questions about your expenses forms and the price of drin and peanuts
Corkscrew	To open wine and frighten the Bulgar maid who, unable to understand the " not disturb" sign you left on the door handle invades your room at 8.15am
Walking stick	To hail taxis; to get a seat on a bus o tube; as protection against cyclists w ride on the pavement at 30 mph and ignore every traffic regulation with impunity
An understanding manager	Shows understanding when you expla that the soup really did cost £8 and th small gin and tonic at the Theatre wa (without the lemon slice)
Air Spray	When the Hotel informs you that "Unfortunately, we have no more non- smoking rooms"
MP3 Player	When there s nothing to watch on TV- usually Tuesdays, Wednesdays and Thursdays.

/S

ı writing a CV it is important to sell yourself in a concise and well laid out

vo pages should usually be enough.

se subheadings

ie font should be easy to read e.g. Arial and the text a good size e.g. 12 pt.

ake your CV stand out from the crowd

st your major achievements and say why you want the work for which you
e applying. Be positive but do not lie.

ollowing are extracts from some famous CVs.

ır Wilde
I want to become a security guard at Tesco
vorking with people. My acquaintances say I am good at small talk. For example
someone departs with a heavily laden trolley full of alcohol, I could say "Ah, yes,
the curse of the drinking classes then if I see a trolley full of cream cakes I might
ıate the customer s day by saying " The only way to get rid of temptation is to yield
lon t you think, chuck?" One can always be kind to people about whom one cares
ıg.

re I see myself in 5 years time
e will flock to my Tesco store, to be the butt of my witticisms and extempore
ks. In gratitude I expect the store to provide me daily with a pink carnation to denote
niority amongst the security guard fraternity. "We are all in the gutter, but some of
looking at the stars". Oh I came out with a good one yesterday "I never put off till
row what I can do the day after, Missus", that one would work well at Tesco.

ies and Pastimes
single man devoted to the nurturing of all things beautiful I spend my time in a state
at awareness, as I only let slip last week at a beastly party I was attending in
avia, "By persistently remaining single, a man converts himself into a permanent
temptation".
a member of many clubs including the Caravan Club.

Alexander the Great

Why I want to become a God King

When we go out drinking, many of my friends say I have the necessary qualities to become a God King. This was confirmed to me when I visited the Oracle[i] of Amun a Siwa. In my travels so far around the Mediterranean, I have been mildly surprised at ingratitude of many of the people I have met, especially the Persians. If I become a King perhaps they will give me a little more respect.

Where I see myself in 5 years time

If I become a God King, I would like to move east to ravage the Persian Empire. I w then conquer Northern India and establish a chain of kebab shops from Athens to D would expect there to be many statues of me, and at least one large city to be name my honour.

Hobbies and Pastimes

Since winning the Macedonian Gymkhana at the age of 4, horses have been my pri and my passion.

Che Guevara

Why I want to be a Salsa Teacher

We Argentinians are born with fire in our bellies and passion in our souls. In my trav around South America, I have noticed that dancing plays a huge part in the lives of ordinary people and now I want to export this fantastic experience to all the peoples the world. As I say, "In Salsa one triumphs or dies". I can also teach Intermediate Ta and basic Merengue.

Where I see myself in 5 years time

I shall become more proficient in Merengue and also learn the Fandango. I will set u Dance school in the heart of Ealing to ensure that no part of the western world is oppressed by the drudgery of the waltz and the military two-step.

Hobbies and Pastimes

I have an extensive collection of berets and they have inspired me to work on a boo entitled "The Beret[ii] — a Social and Political History". I also have a luxuriant beard a keeping that in tip-top condition takes much of my spare time.

[i] On his way to visit the Oracle in the Egyptian desert at Siwa, Alexander and his companions got lost in a sandst believes they were saved from death by a talking bird that led them to their destination. The 2005 Oliver Stone mov Alexander is widely believed to have failed because of the inept performance of the talking bird.

[ii] The beret is the national hat of the French people, typically worn by French artists. Artist s berets are extremely large the sun out of their eyes. Prince had a hit with Raspberry Beret about a girl (possible French) with a beret she mig bought in a second had store.

ent Van Gough

I want to be a plasterer

lly, I wanted to be a painter and decorator but my teacher, Herr Kopenhull, said I s used too much paint and that the punters they would not stand for it. If I am ssful in my application I would like you to consider my mate Paul[iii] who would like to rickie.

e I see myself in 5 years time

ave ambitions to be a painter and decorator so I will probably go to evening s at the Technical College to see if I can cut down on the paint. In five year s I expect to have a Golf Gti.

ies and Pastimes

d to paint watercolours but I got so mad with the colours running that I nearly cut my f (don t ask me why I chose my ear). Paul and I are big Ajax fans and we go to all their matches home and away.

rt Einstein[iv]

I want to become a jockey

always been fond of horses. They are creatures that uniquely amongst the animal om can travel very quickly with a human on their back. I am working on a theory that e on a very fast beast I may be able to enter another dimension or at least win a s race at Plumpton.

re I see myself in 5 years time

ends what you mean by time . If time is like a spongy melon, as I predict, then I be having tea with President Lincoln or playing in the world snooker championship 6. Then again I might be cleaning out the stable yard with my fellow workers.

ies and Pastimes

time indeed "pass"? Does it not have physical qualities like hair or cheese? If time ore does not pass but rather change in form and dimension, should not the question rased, Hobbies? Is work a hobby? Is not my life, my work my hobby? Who knows? is so much we do not know that I must investigate.

robably refers to his friend Paul C zanne with whom Vincent had a tempestuous relationship. Their rivalry can be ack to school bricklaying lesson when there was a furious row over who had built the better Flemish Bond. Most oraries agree that it was Paul because Vincent used too much mortar.

was a student in Zurich where the best place to eat is a restaurant in a converted armoury called Zeughauskeller. It own whether Albert ate there.

Sir Lawrence Olivier[V]

Why I want to be a tour guide

Darlings, consider the majesty of my oration as I surmount the stage that is the uppe deck of my Big London Tour Bus. I confound the excesses of cruel nature, as I launc into fulsome praise as we first espy Wren s masterpiece, St Paul s. Consider yet the pathos I shall evoke as we pass Tyburn and I recall the horrors and humiliations of tl noble martyrs, who were so viciously done to death by hanging, and mutilation, very to the Kentucky Fried Chicken emporium.

Where I see myself in 5 years time

In this business, dear boy, who can tell? I might have progressed to a comfortable, a conditioned coach, where I could declaim to ruddy-faced Russian tourists. Alternativ might be alone, yes entirely alone, atop a 243 bus lamenting the fates that have now cruelly turned on me and pressed their icy blades into my vulnerable and defenceles shell — *sic transit Gloria*; who can tell?

Hobbies and Pastimes

In my chosen profession, it is terribly, terribly important to research. With ambitions t have such an important role, it would be remiss of me not to check the succulence o pies at the Dog and Partridge in Barnes from time to time, and sample the fries at McDonalds and Burger King on a regular basis.

Josef Stalin

Why I want to be a priest

I am a humble man. I love people and want to help them to be happy. I believe that t happiness will not be found in this world and that we should help people to leave for greater, permanent destination. In fact in this life many people should not seek happ at all, rather a period of atonement in cold and inhospitable places that can only impr the soul. I have a great moustache.

Where I see myself in 5 years time

I shall take great care of my moustache to ensure that it stays firm and clean. I shall ensure that my flock are regularly reminded that this life is nasty brutal and short anc their backbreaking work is necessary to ensure stability and equality in this life, and t glory of salvation in the next.

Hobbies and Pastimes

When I am not praying, I imagine what it would be like to live in the cold and rugged wastelands of Siberia. I sometimes go into my garden and pretend to be a hermit livi such an unforgiving place.[vii]

[V] Lawrence was born in Dorking, Surrey. If you visit Dorking you can find out more about the area from a small inform board situated in The Old Kings Head Court opposite the Nat West Bank

[vii] Stalin has a problem with his real name-Josif Vissarionovich Dzhugashvili. As a priest he would get away with Fath but to be on the safe side he has chosen an easy to remember name.

ɔrence Nightingale

ıy I want to be an International Lawyer

an ex-nurse I am well used to dealing with inadequate people who are in desperate ɘd. I also feel I would be good with your clients. As my name suggests I was born in y and have considerable experience of other foreign countries including the Ukraine. I n lamps that I can use in countries with uncertain supplies of electricity.

ıere I see myself in 5 years time

tend to shine my light (excuse my play on words) into the many murky areas of ɘrnational Law, such as the thousand year old dispute between Turkmenistan, ɘrbaijan and Uzbekistan about the ownership of three (long deceased) stray sheep and long-standing claims of the people of Croydon[vii] to drive their cattle through the streets Boulogne on market days.

bbies and Pastimes

ntaining my large lamp collection takes up a great deal of my time.
ve recently joined the Badminton Club and Weightwatchers.

yphus

y I want to work in IT Procurement

a former King of Corinth, I have experience of work on several large government racts. Lately, I have become involved with logistics and in particular the movement of avy ball up a hill.I have on many occasions almost succeeded in my task only to be arted at the last moment by an unforeseen act of spite by someone in authority[viii] (an nowable contingency as I see it). I feel that this background leads me to be uniquely ɘd for the advertised role.

ɘre I see myself in 5 years time

expectation of near success that is dashed by a last minute change of specification or ess will leave me unfazed. I will consequently be able to hide the collective bitter ppointment rather well, and I shall still invite the team to go-carting and paint balling petitions to celebrate our milestones.

bies and Pastimes

ever-ending quest to move the heavy ball up a steep hill will continue to occupy any time.

cally there are now no cattle in Croydon. The council banned them, along with Capuchin Monkeys and zebras, in r causing a nuisance to the residents in the Bradmore Green area.

phus is currently being punished by the Gods for murder, illegal detention and other crimes. He should really have ıed these on his CV. Check with your HR Dept if you are not sure about disclosure of these types of misdemeanour.

Diego Maradona

Why I want to become a Basketball Player

Although many of my friends joke that I am a midget[ix], I believe that in my career I have shown the ability to scale great heights and influence important events. This has been done with the assistance of God. I can see no reason why this assistance will not be there when I need it and I am sure that my fans will flock to see me play for your team.

Where I see myself in 5 years time

I shall be the toast of the USA. I shall have scored more points than Michael Jordan. I will be more famous than all the Harlem Globetrotters put together, Argentina will be the Olympic champions. With God s help I cannot fail.

Hobbies and Pastimes

I love food, God has given me the ability to consume vast quantities of food and it does not affect my weight. If I eat more I shall grow taller and become an even greater Basketball player.

Napoleon Bonaparte

Why I want to become a European Commissioner

As you may have read I have suffered for my dedication to the European cause, and t countries that surround France seem to have taken a personal dislike to me. Notwithstanding their ingratitude, I feel that I have much to offer the real challenges fa by the Commission such as why all Brussels pate should be made in Belgium and agreeing on the date when Kent and East Sussex become part of Normandy.

Where I see myself in 5 years time

As my position requires, I shall be resident in a large Palace in the vicinity of Brussels (not Waterloo[x]). I will have harmonised the English and soon I shall be making my mo on Russia. You see I have learnt from my past mistakes.

Hobbies and Pastimes

I am the member of several clubs and societies including the Pony Club and the Brus Operatic Society.

I also keep tropical fish.

[ix] Earl Boykins of the Denver Nuggets is just 5'5" tall. Maradona is half an inch taller.

[x] The French defeat at Waterloo has recently been ascribed to an impetuous cavalry officer who tried to storm the En squares too early and was followed by other hotheaded French cavalrymen. This was not mentioned in the Abba's 19 recording of the battle.

vig Van Beethoven

I want to be an ice cream salesman

' life I have been interested in music. I often wake in the middle of the night ing a tune that has come to me in my sleep. If I am successful in my application I e so happy to be playing nice melodies to attract the children to my Mr Whippy van ' their "99s"[xiii] and Raspberry Ripples. My favourite song is Greensleeves and I 'e I would play that one very many times.

re I see myself in 5 years time

s time of global warming, I have no doubt that this is an ideal time to be entering the eam business. Ideally I would like to be in charge of three or four vans on a large e. I would very much like the opportunity to be in control of the music played by vans to attract the children.

ies and Pastimes

/ beer. I make sausages. I play bridge. I have a collection of wigs. I try to write :.

atma[xiv] Ghandi

I want to be a Bouncer

ugh I am slight of stature, I have developed methods to overcome those who do not with my point of view. My experience in ending the occupation of my country by the powerful Imperial force in history will stand me in good stead if I get the opportunity doorman at the Pig and Ferret during Happy Hour on a busy Saturday after the derby. I am confident that my passive resistance techniques will have the desired on the binge drinkers of Glasgow.

re I see myself in 5 years time

s than five years time I will have eliminated raucous behaviour on the streets of ow. It is my mission to take my methods of passive resistance and constructive gement to other cities and towns such as Middlesborough and St Albans where is great need of calm and reconciliation.

ies and Pastimes

/ spare time is devoted to the spread of peace and harmony and improving my skills e billiard table.

rding to Cadbury, Italian monarchs had an elite guard consisting of 99 soldiers. As many Italians sold ice-cream they d ice cream with a flake as a '99' something that was special or first class.

'th, Ghandi was given the name Mohandas Karamchand Ghandi, only later did he become known as Mahatma (great term of respect for a Brahmin sage. On CV's make use of honorary titles and awards although it is considered vulgar an inhertied title, unless appling for a job in the USA.

The Moon

Why I want to be a planet

I feel I am in a rut. I have been going round in circles for the past thirty billion years (least that is what it feels like). I am sure that I now have the experience and skills to the Sun or some other large star. I know I am only small, but size isn t everything, an have been told that I am very good with tides[xi]. Please do not be influenced by Were stories, as they are myths.

Where I see myself in 5 years time

I shall be getting used to my new orbit. If I am not sure of the area I shall report to m territory manager. I want to be a planet to be proud of and not the subject of jokes ab cheese and lunatics. Perhaps I shall colour myself yellow and become affectionately known as the "Yellow" planet — or maybe crimson. I want earthlings to speculate endlessly about whether I contain water and am I made of rock or gas.

Hobbies and Pastimes

Astronomy and collecting space junk

Lassie

Why I want the role of Spider-Dog

For many years I have played an active role in saving the lives of children and old pe from forest fires, flooded caves, landslides and the like. Sometimes I have helped to apprehend villains who in many cases where responsible for these catastrophes. I no feel I am ready to be the world s first superhero canine. I am not afraid of heights and happy to wear costumes[xii].

Where I see myself in 5 years time

After Spider Dog 4 I shall need a rest, as by then I will be nearing burn out. It is my ambition to star with Jennifer Anniston in a gentle romantic comedy, or become a rov UN Ambassador like Michael Jackson or Angelina Jolie. Ultimately, I see myself as a writer and director.

Hobbies and Pastimes

When I not filming I relax in my caravan by playing on my Playstation2. I collect rug squeaky toys, and unusually shaped biscuits

[xi] The best time to catch fish is when a full or new moon is rising or setting.

[xii] Lassie is in fact a male dog! This clearly poses a dilema for his CV entry. I advise that he makes it clear that he is m avoid any problems with first impressions if invited to an interview. He should insert a section about why he has playe female role. 'Tootsie' and 'Mrs. Doubtfire' did not seem to adversely affect Dustin Hoffman or Robin Williams.

ne Mongol Hordes

hy we want to be taxi drivers

be perfectly frank we are unhappy with our current manager (Genghis). He makes us e small horses for days on end from one part of China[xv] to the other, killing people as go. It is a very hazardous profession and there is often wanton disregard for health d safety. What is more the food is lousy. Were we to become taxi drivers, we would preciate the warmth of our vehicles, and the chance to stop regularly for fish and chips. would be prepared to travel south of the river after 8.00 p.m. (except weekends)

ere we see ourselves in 5 years time

5 years we expect to have put deposits on holiday villas in Spain. Some of us want to in Minorca but the majority of the Horde prefers Benidorm. No way are we going back ve off dried yak s milk on the deserts and grasslands of our youth, roaming around that madman Genghis.

bbies and Pastimes

often meet at our club to talk about the old days and the things we got up to. We ned a polo team, but were unfairly barred from the league, which accused us of being aggressive and the cause of several fatalities. We now feel that polo is institutionally st and have taken the Hurlingham Club to the Equal Opportunities Commission - we cipate significant compensation.

nghis Khan

y I want to be Food Scientist

some time I have had the feeling that my staff have been unhappy with my forceful ership style. I think that this is a result of the enormous quantities of dried yak milk they have had to consume on our field trips. With more knowledge of food science aps I can motivate them with more interesting culinary experiences and, therefore, d so many public executions.

ere I see myself in 5 years time

a happy and well-fed Horde behind me I can become the undisputed leader of the vn world. I shall also write a cookery book to advise future Horde leaders of the best es to ensure motivation and a balanced diet. My ultimate goal is to become a prity chef.

bies and Pastimes

icking, drinking, fishing[xvi], cake-decoration and torture.

Hordes once tried to invade Japan but the army perished at sea in a typhoon, a Divine Wind as the Japanese saw it Kaze

nghis murdered his brother Bektair when he was only eleven because Bektair had stolen a fish that Genghis had Best leave this sort of thing off CV unless you have been comvicted (even then check with your Probation Officer disclosure)

Leonardo da Vinci

Why I want to play for Juventus

You may know me from the many pictures I have painted not to mention my inventions, and general all round genius. However, for any red bloodied Italian man there is no greater honour than to be seen emerging from the Stadio Delle Alpi dressed from head toe in the best from Versace after nodding in the decider in the match against the *cretir* from Inter Milan.

Where I see myself in 5 years time

Should I stay in football? I don t know. Maybe I shall design a new rocket or a machine making better pasta shapes — anything could happen with a brain like mine. Maybe I need a good woman who can keep me focussed — perhaps a strong German woman c do that. World watch out, the best of Leonardo is yet to come!

Hobbies and Pastimes

A genius has no need for hobbies. Pastimes are for wimps.
However, I am the Grand Master of the Priory of Sion[xxii]. (I cannot talk about this)

The Aztecs

Why we want to be Cossacks

For a long time we have indulged in bloodletting and blood sacrifice. We now recognis that this is often unfair and discriminates against slaves, ethnic minorities and neighbouring cultures. We have noticed that the Ukrainian Cossacks have a proud tradition of independence and we are impressed with your diversity and equal opportunities policies. If we are allowed to join the Cossacks we will bring with us competencies in gardening and temple building in swampy lands. We will integrate mu better than the wimpy Incas who only want to emigrate to avoid climbing high mountai every day and eating leaves and roots[xvii].

Where we see ourselves in 5 years time

Within 5 years we will have built at least four large temples on the banks of the Dniep We will start to cultivate cocoa, and consider adopting the Orthodox faith. We will bec integrated in the ways of the Cossack and if asked we shall return to our bloody tradit to protect the life and liberty of the people of the Ukraine.

Hobbies and Pastimes

Needlework, basket weaving and flower arranging.

[xxii] Membership of secret societies is not necessarily a problem for professional footballer's. Seek advice from your ag avoid unfortunate leaks to the tabloids. The last thing you want to read on a Monday morning is 'Juve striker in Son of Shock!"

[xvii] It is best not to denigrate other applicants. This is a sigh of insecurity and negativity. Even if it is true that the Incas wimps, it is good to be neutral about differences but concentrate on your strengths.

r John Betjeman

hy I want to be Rudyard Kipling

nd in the sandwiches and wasps in the jam
e regiment marches through Afghanistan
ck through the Transvaal, summoned by bells
e mongoose[xix] *hunts snakes, and saves Tunbridge Wells*

his the sort of thing you want?

at I see myself writing in 5 years time

me friendly bombs and fall on Lucknow
natives are in a mood right now
major snores but the Empire roars
"It's gins all round" on Trebetherick's shores

s is how my verse might develop

bbies and Pastimes

en I m not trainspotting, I catalogue my interesting collection of pipes.

e Terminator

y I want to be an oven

get older I feel that I am an obsolete design for the purpose for which I was originally gned. Younger and faster machines can now eliminate life far more quickly than I could. I have a rubbish pension scheme. I have seen it wasted on narcotics by evil rg designers. I now find I have to work into old age. Therefore, I would greatly value opportunity to be an oven. I enjoy the smell of bread and roast chicken but would r not to work with fish.[xx]

ere I see myself in 5 years time

ars is enough for any oven. Once again I shall become an obsolete machine. I think I e happy with life in the kitchen and so becoming a toaster or a microwave is what I d desire. I would not like to become a toasted sandwich maker, as I want to perform eful function.

bies and Pastimes

sh myself. I learn a new language (English)

mongoose referred to is likely to be a Javan mongoose that is famous for killing snakes, especially the venomous Mongooses are not immune to snake venom; rather they strike quickly to avoid being bitten.

y people believe that Borg from Star Trek and Robocop are true cyborgs whilst Terminator is more of a robot. or Peter Fromhertz at the Max Planck Institute in Martinsried, near Munich, is conducting experiments where he has o nerves to microchips - scary or what?

Fidel Castro

Why I want to be a Bingo Caller

For many years now my doctor has been telling me to take life more easily. A part-time job like this would be ideal. I have much experience in talking to large crowds for sever hours, and so taking four evening sessions at the Gala Club in South Shields should no prove problematic. I have learnt all the calls; thirty three - two fat ladies , clackety-clack and so on.[xxi]

Where I see myself in 5 years time

Do they have bingo in Las Vegas? I am not so sure. If they do my dream would be to t my luck in Sin City. If that was not an option, I could perhaps become a celebrity caller and do the rounds of all the Gala clubs in the North East of England. For this I would need a chauffeur, as I do not drive too well. Perhaps I could be working on a cruise shi but probably not out of Miami.

Hobbies and pastimes

My life over the past few years has been increasingly consumed by Bingo. I collect Bir paraphernalia and I am writing a history of Bingo 1530 - 1776. Did you know that whe was first introduced into the USA, winners would shout "Beano" and not "Bingo"?

Adolf Hitler

Why I want to become a Member of the European Parliament.

For many years I have had a passionate interest in European unity. If I am nominated become an MEP I will take all steps necessary to fulfil my dream of a prosperous Eurc a peaceful Europe and the unity of the peoples of Europe[xxii] (excluding of course, Sla gypsies, Jews, Muslims, Bolsheviks, cripples, left handed people, and anyone with a funny look).

Where I see myself in 5 years time

The Common Fisheries Policy Directive Number 433/5 concerning the spawning peric of sand eels in the waters around Heligoland has long been a source of friction betwe those who fish in those waters. I promise, that if the issue is not resolved quickly, the Danish fishing fleet must realise that I cannot be held responsible for the measures th will be taken to ensure that German *fischervolk* are given their rightful access to thes waters; waters to which Destiny has bequeathed to us an undisputed historical claim.

Hobbies and Pastime

I enjoy socialising in my castle. I am the reigning Southern Bavarian yodelling champ race pigeons. I also like painting, writing and studying anthropology.

[xxi]Bingo calls should rhyme; for 87 it is 'Torquay in Devon' and for 79 it is 'One More Time'. Castro should note that 33 'Dirty Knee'. Always check your facts if you want that interview.

[xxii] Adolf has a sister in law, Brigid Hitler, who lived in Toxteth in Liverpool. She claims that he visited there in 1912. Ir War II Liverpool was extensively bombed by the Luftwaffe.

Archbishop of Canterbury

I want to become a Druid.

since I took over this job, I have been assailed by a litany of problems. Should n become Bishops? Should homosexuals become Bishops? Should our egation in Ghana secede before our friends in Massachusetts? Is there a God? d the Reverend Turner in Middle Wallop buy a new carpet for the vicarage? How supposed to deal with all these matters? As a druid nobody will care what I think, I wander around Stonehenge at mid-summer chanting as I go, and look impressive ny robes and my fine beard and then go home and commune with my bees.

re I see myself in 5 years time

sage that the life of a druid will become increasingly popular over the next few years established church tears itself to pieces. There is a danger that people will then o me for guidance about carpets and beard length, so I can see myself applying for ncy in one of the Dunhuang caves in Central China.

ies and Pastime

to talk to my bees[xxiii]. Otherwise I listen to Bach (any of them will do).

am Shakespeare

I want to become a Rap Artist and Celebrity DJ

been told that I must connect with a younger, more ethnically diverse audience to e that I keep my Arts Council grant. Consequently my future plays will reflect my ciation of the struggles within the black ghettos of cities in the United States of ca. This is the opening of one of my new adaptations, called M. C. Beth[xxiv].

er and lightening, enter three witches
se women are wicked bitches
reeps up on me with your knives to my Lexus
oothe, I will say 'bout Banquo that he don't respect us

re I see myself in 5 years time

year s time the ghettos will be alive to the rythm of another ethnic group, so it be unwise for me to jeopardise my grant by trying to be too precise in my tions. I am, however, starting to become familiar with the rhythms and cultures iated with Bhatiali river songs from Bangladesh.

ies and Pastime

as to take a keen interest in politics and fashion. I read GQ and the NME.

r of bees is called apiphobia. Four percent of people are allergic to bee stings. There are 20,124 varieties of bee. In kies more people are killed by bees than by bears.

ne members of the Scottish parliament feel that Macbeth was an enlightened monarch who would no more incite and deal in Black Magic than would Bambi.

The Glittering Path (Dao-Ji)

Many have found contentment in paying large amounts of money to training organisa
to gain an awareness of how their minds and bodies react, or could react, to differen
situations. These courses authorise the participants to bore their colleagues with jarg
and amaze them with profound statements of the obvious, at work and / or at social
events.

There follows, the key tenets of the, almost forgotten, ancient Chinese philosophy of
Glittering Path (Dao-Ji).

By reading this page once you will become a Practitioner.

By reading this page twice you will become a Master Practitioner.

If you read this page three times you will transcend *The Glittering Path* of the Sevent
Sigma to reach a state of Dao-Ji.

Terminology	What it means for you
You-Wu	*Being-Non-being.* When things change do they cease to exist? When someone borrows your mouse mat and forgets to return it, do you not remember the original hurt? Buy them a cream cake and make a virtue of a potential conflict.
Shi-Fei	*This–Not* Often we are stressed at work because of a difference of opinion; however, we are usually looking for the same outcome and we both get paid at the end of the month. As the Beatles put it, I say Hello (shi) and you say Goodbye (fei) So chill!
Dao	Dao has no literal English translation but there are many uses for the concept e.g. The Way we were; Do you know the Way to San Hose? W out West; My Way; On our Way home; Do you know the way to the photocopier? Use Dao when you get lost.
Wu-Wei	A paradox Do something but do not regard it as important. We are ofter faced with that irritating task at month end when we compile those repo that no one ever looks at. Do not be worried by your actions as no one cares what your report says; only why was it written.
Qing	*Reality/feelings* Not the irritation of waiting for a Northern Line train at Bank Station on a hot July evening. This refers to the need for pot plant your office. It suggests that you need a harmonious environment and yo should not over water your Monstera deliciosa or Spider plants or they go pale and lose their leaves and vigour.
Yi-Ren	*Moral-Benevolent* All office behaviour should be imbued with this conce The implication is that managers should never let flirtations get out of control, and that they should regularly take their staff to a decent Chine restaurant for a full banquet.

(How I became) SuperBrian

me is Brian. I recently had two weeks to prepare an important presentation.

is my story...

ay 12th May

the cat, clean the car, go to the tip and there was something else. Cut the grass? vas like a swamp out there; collect Ruth from Wendy s? No she s at Suki s till ow. Oh yes, it was that bloody presentation a week on Friday.

to present to Global Utilities, on how we could improve their all round customer care bought our exciting new customer contact software, Call-it.

ouble was, apart from when I my brother got married, I hadn t presented since I was versity. Then it was forty minutes of private terror and communal boredom as I ned, with the help of twenty-five acetates, the impact on Anglo — French relations of bulent life and lamentable death of Edward the Second. Stupid topic, now I come k.

ving grace on that damp Sunday afternoon was that later in the week I had the e to observe some of my esteemed colleagues in action. I could check out what id and then substitute my script and slides. What a brilliant plan!

day 14th May

ay had been a disaster, Nigel Cray, my graduate trainee handed in his notice saying s off to Nepal to work for rice and leaves teaching peasants to speak English. Fat good he d do there, he was far better employed here monitoring my budgets and wonderful things with spreadsheets. Then Julie, the new clerk, dropped her coffee ne of our servers and we were in disaster recovery mode all day.

day, my plan would start to take shape. I went to the Boardroom to hear a ntation by Jimmy Mullet the Personnel Officer. Jimmy couldn t wait to get out of the any, and the recent reorganisation, the subject of his talk, was to be his last.

arrived, we sat in rows facing a screen flanked by avant garde pictures emented with fatuous corporate messages (there s no I in Team etc.). A large potted on the right of the stage gave an unlikely hint of the tropics. Through the window to ght of the screen I could see trees and fields.
y had been with the company since week two. I had heard him present before and ever really analysed his style. Even though I remembered nothing of his previous pts, I was of the opinion that anyone who had the guts to present deserved some f support,

I sat, pen in hand, to make notes so I could learn from a master.

Jimmy stood, he cleared his throat with a loud harrumph, his eyes turned to David F Director of Operations and he spoke. "As you know my name is ".

After saying something about the good old days when Personnel Officers were giver more respect, and how he missed old Mrs Haddock the former tea lady, and his drea golfing on the Algarve for the rest of his life, he put an acetate on the Overhead Proj

The acetate represented, or so Jimmy said, the complete restructure plan.

His slide was a masterpiece in black and white. If displayed at the Tate Modern it wo have been pondered over for many a year. The Guardian Art critic might comment u "its genuflection to the early inclinations of a younger Miro" whilst the Sun would hav said, "mad, bad and sad".

From where I sat I could not read a word.

Jimmy meanwhile was shuffling from foot to foot still looking at an increasingly embarrassed David Fish. His words floated around the room but disappeared from consciousness before they reached their targets. I tried to spot the changes to my department in the plan but could not decide if the arrows coming from our departmer box were good arrows or bad arrows.

For the next twenty-five minutes my pen, poised to list Jimmy s good points, stayed unused except for the little picture of a desert island that the palm had inspired. Long before Jimmy s deputy, Roger Dolphin asked a sycophantic, probably planted questic had drifted into a near coma and had planned the ten records I would take to my des island. (Grace — Jeff Buckley, Court and Spark - Joni Mitchell, Messiah — Handel, Revolver — Beatles, Gaucho — Steely Dan, Blonde on Blonde — Bob Dylan, Gold - Ry Adams, The Band — The Band, and greatest hits from Jackson Browne, and Neil You

Jimmy s notes kindly provided on the company Intranet allowed me the chance to wo out the significance of the arrows but what did I learn from Jimmy s presentation?

What I learnt from Jimmy's presentation

- Beware of distractions. The palm tree encouraged me to think about the tropics, not topics. The pictures and window also distracted me.
- If you stare at one person it is uncomfortable for the subject of your gaze and turns off the rest of the audience
- The visual aids must be simple and readable
- Words alone are of little value, especially if they are if not well delivered and supported

t to worry, I thought. My expectations of learning from Jimmy had never been that high, d later that week I had the chance to listen to Sally Bream who was to address a group Chinese engineers about the success of our joint venture in Shanghai.

ednesday 15th May
boss, a gruff Yorkshireman by the name of Paul Pickering, popped his head round my bicle. "That presentation ready yet?"

coming on" I lied.

ursday 16th May
Chinese engineers led by their leader Mr Baiji, trooped into conference room one for y Bream s presentation. They all wore newly acquired Next raincoats that had bably been made within miles of their homes and they all dutifully carried a company stic bag full of glossy brochures that Public Relations could not dump on anyone else.

d high hopes for this presentation as Sally was seen as a "bright young thing" in the s of some important people as she had been to private school and Oxford. She didn t k so much as bounce around the office, smiling at all the right people and saying solutely" a lot.

e enough she began by saying "How absolutely wonderful it is to have the opportunity peak to our friends, the delegation from ".

n down went the lights and on went the projector. Mr Baiji and his colleagues then erienced forty-five minutes of PowerPoint torture.

-four slides were launched. They appeared from the left, from the right, from the top, the bottom, even from the middle. There were slides with graphs, slides with text, s with cartoon people and slides with mysterious flow charts. There were slides e the cartoon people took over the flow charts to the sound of boxes disappearing to ound of explosions.

was up there somewhere. I glimpsed her at the side of the platform earnestly sing away at her laptop and checking that her cartoon army appeared on cue. She d flustered and uncomfortable; she spoke like a berserk machine gun; her feet never ped moving. The air was full of incomprehensible phrases such as " the emergency warehousing contingency will continue to be addressed by our integration strategy ", argon " our forthcoming IPO will resolve all R and D issues in the NPD". Each time lrew breath, Sally would throw in an "erm" an "actually" and of course lots of olutelys". No more was this the bounding Sally, with confidence to spare, this was a d, intimidated Sally - mistress of the machine, slave to the sound bite.
Chinese looked on inscrutably. Occasionally one would break ranks and glimpse at

the annual report or the booklet proclaiming our export successes in Bolivia, but they invariably refocused to stare politely at the colourful images passed for a "presentation

At the end when a flushed, breathless and deflated Sally asked for questions, there wa an uncomfortable silence, until Mr Baiji politely enquired about the number of graduates the company employed each year. Sally finished by thanking the bewildered group for attending and true to form, hoped that the rest of their stay would be "absolutely fantas

What I learned from Sally:

- Even seemingly confident people can be nervous and withdrawn when facing an audience
- PowerPoint when badly used can cause very serious problems
- An effective speaker needs to be seen to be in command
- The needs and level of the audience should be checked before (and during the presentation)
- Audiences need to be entertained

As Mr Baiji stood, the smiles returned to the eyes of the audience as they contemplate their lunch. Before they left, Mr Baiji said a few words in broken English. In a slow pac he thanked Sally for the effort she had made and felt sure that with such energetic pe the joint venture was in safe hands. I do not know what he was thinking.
I had a week to prepare and my brilliant plan (to steal the ideas of others) was in tatte

Friday 17th May

What I learned from Mr Baiji:

- The speaker does not need to betray their thoughts
- Speaking slowly allows you to consider you thoughts and appear composed

A big problem arose with one of our servers. Spent all day trying to retrieve vital data time to think about anything else.

Got home tired and stressed. I slumped in front of the television with bottle of wine ar felt sorry for myself.
Lots of old rubbish on television. But two of my old favourites cheered me up. First th was an old Bilko Show. He always made me laugh, Maybe it was his quick fire gags, maybe his expressions and movements. Bilko s face always seemed to reveal the humour before the words.

en there was Frasier. The entire cast worked well together, the writing was always :ellent and I could empathise with the central character who could never get his life ıctly as he hoped it would be.

fore bedtime, as I sipped my cocoa and thought about my week, some glimmers of ıt began to appear about my presentation thanks to the unlikely trio of Sergeant Bilko, sier and Mr Baiji.
lt a glimmer of hope.

Vhat I learned from Sergeant Bilko and Frasier Crane:

Both comedians allowed me time to absorb their material — it seems to be true that the secret of great comedy is timing
So much of their messages came through their faces. Bilko would reduce the audience to tears without speaking and Frasier s face always supported his, usually pained, emotions
What you say is often not terribly important. How you say your words is always very important

urday 18th May

ke up feeling positive. I was definitely going to draft out my talk today.

ldy, daddy, can we go swimming to-day?"
me later, would you Ruth?"

minutes later.

ldy, daddy can we go swimming today?"
..alright then."

'hat I learned from Ruth:
Have a simple objective
Don t be afraid to repeat your key points

feeding the cat, going to the baths, a trip to the tip and cutting the grass, I had little to prepare my presentation before it was time to meet my best friend Ben in his local Frantic Ferret". Ben had opinions about everything. When I told him about my ntation, he told me all sorts of weird things that happened to the body when it was r stress. He said I would lose my appetite, fidget, and sway from side to side, want to the toilet, look like the cat had died and sweat like a pig.

"How do you know all this? I asked"

"I saw your best man s speech, remember? Anyway don t feel too bad about it, lots of famous people, actors, politicians, all sorts of people get like that. Usually they cover it really well, that s cause they re actors I suppose. Anyway all you need to do is tell wha you re going to tell em; tell em; and then tell em what you ve told em "

What I learned from Ben:

- It is natural to exhibit signs of nerves
- Almost everyone suffers from nerves
- Nerves need not be apparent to the audience
- Build a simple structure

Sunday 19th May
I have fed the cat, read the papers, prepared lunch. I have time to make a start on my presentation.

I began by thinking about my audience. I expected six people to be present including Martin Chubb, Customer Services Director, and Lisa Tench, IT Director. They would be from a variety of backgrounds with a mixture of technical understanding.

I decided to be clear about my purpose; **"To persuade Global Utilities that ou customer contact software will improve the efficiency of their custon services department".**

I knew I needed a beginning — my introduction; a middle — my main sections, and an — the summary.

One of the lessons I learned from Sally was not to cram in eleven sections.
After several attempts I built a simple structure. It had four sections.

1. An overview of the company
2. Our analysis of Global's needs
3. The features of the software
4. The benefits to Global

That did not take as long as I thought and as I took my old sofa to the tip I reviewed progress with a faint glow of satisfaction and considered if there are any key points th the structure would not allow me to include. **I considered their likely question**

There were four days to go to the presentation but I had made a start and I felt pleas that I had the foundations on which I could build.

ay 20th May

hrimpton, my Departmental Training advisor said I should log on to the company s et to get help with the presentation, she said there was a wonderful E-Learning site old you all about presenting. Her suggestion was in response to me being negative , and moaning that my talk would be terrible and I d probably lose my job after my ntation to Global and end up collecting trolleys at the supermarket. Despite my ve feelings of yesterday, there were still huge gaps in my self-confidence.

ntranet site helped a little. It advised me to keep it simple; to start with impact and ith a summary. It suggested that I involve the audience wherever possible. Crucially, me never to talk myself down, and that during the presentation I would be the r.

ough lunch, as I munched on my tuna and tomato sandwich, I told myself "I am the r, I am the leader".

ed at my budding plan again. I revised my structure so that I could start in a way ould make a good impression and end in a way that allowed me to repeat my key s.

must begin by raising expectations and setting out how the talk will be delivered.

introduction I decided that there should be five elements:

. "killer" fact and/or a prop with lots of impact
n important reason why they needed to listen to me
he time I would take to tell them
Vhen they could respond
he outline of my structure

ish I would to summarise my main key points.
vised structure looked like this:

duction

verview of the company

analysis of Global's needs

features of the software

benefits

mary

on a roll. I was happy with my structure and knew how to start and finish. I decided ntinue by listing the key points I was to cover in each section.

Introduction

- Impact: Universal Utilities (main rival) has growth target of 25% next fiscal year
- Need: Our product Call-it has proven capacity to retain customers
- Time: I shall speak for 25 minutes
- Response: There will be time for questions at the end
- Outline: I shall cover - **Overview of the company**
Analysis of Global's needs
Features of the software
Benefits of Call-it

Section 1: Overview of the Company

- Formed in early nineties
- Employing 500 skilled staff
- Clients include
- World-wide presence in every continent
- 24/7 Help desk

Section 2: Analysis of Global's need

- Market for services to grow by 50% per year
- Increased competition (especially Universal)
- Staff retention issues in customer department
- Desire to promote itself as a global player

Section 3: Features of the Call-it software

- Ease of use
- Accommodates ERP software
- Well proven
- Market leader

Section 4: Benefits of Call-it

- Allows cross selling of Global services
- Fast-track training of staff
- Less data storage requirements
- Speediest product on market

Summary

- We have been in business for fifteen years and have over four hundred large and repeat customers etc.
- We have assessed Global s likely needs and I have outlined the systems that ma your need
- The features of our systems that will help users and customers are
- The bottom line benefits to Global will be

iting down the key points associated with each section only took half an hour and when
uff Paul Pickering put his head round the corner of my cubicle to ask me how things
re going, I could honestly say "Not bad, thanks Paul"

I had to do now, I thought, was think about my slides.

esday 21st May

I approached the shining glass construction that was Call-it House something was
hering me. Had I fed Basil the cat? Cats are resourceful I thought, he ll think of
nething, I hoped it would not be a blackbird. But there was something else.

on after I arrived, I met with Jonathan Dory the Sales and Marketing Director who was
co-present with me at Global. We talked in general about our content and he gave me
ne information about the "company standard" for slides.

en he had gone my nagging worry emerged. It was the slides.

membered Jimmy with his obscure arrows and boxes and I remembered poor Sally
am who lost her audience, lost the argument and lost her renowned self-confidence
using all those explosive, exhausting and excruciating slides. I remembered all those
able, wasted hours over the last few years when I had daydreamed and fantasised,
one useless slide driven presentation followed another equally useless, equally slide
en presentation.

re must be a better way.

r coffee I began to list possible alternatives to a totally slide driven presentation.
ist included:

Demonstration
Audience participation
Quotes
Anecdotes / Stories
Examples
Pictures
Use of Whiteboard / Flip Chart
Rhetorical questions
Exercises
Video / Audio
Props
Me!

y of these would not be appropriate for the Global presentation, but I began to feel
by using some of the above my presentation could even be entertaining.
n re-considered my structure and key points and began to link some of the above to

what I wanted the audience to remember:

For my thirty minutes, I would have no more than four or five slides and most of those would consist of graphs or pictures (e.g. a map showing our international offices). I wou include a demonstration, audience participation, a prop, success stories, examples, and plenty of opportunities to assess the audience.

SECTION	**SUPPORT**
INTRO Impact, Need, Time, Response, Outline structure	Prop 3G mobile Slide to outline structure
Section 1: Overview of the Company • Formed in early nineties • Employing 500 skilled staff • Clients include • World-wide presence in every continent • 24/7 Help desk	Brief story about work with Swiss Bank in Zurich Map showing location of clients Picture of Help Desk in action
Section 2: Analysis of Global's need • Market for services to grow by 50% per year • Increased competition (especially Universal) • Staff retention issues in customer department • Desire to promote itself as world player	Graph showing our understanding of market growth Quotes from Global annual report. Rhetorical questions
Section 3: Features of the Call-it software • Ease of use • Integrates ERP / bespoke products • Well proven • Market leader	Demonstration of Call-it Ask for volunteer to operate laptop Display on screen
Section 4: Benefits of Call-it Global • Allows cross selling of Global services • Fast-track training of staff • Less data storage requirements • Speediest product on market	Examples of benefits (2 brief case studies) Estimates of cost savings on slide
Summary	Repeat key points Ask for questions

I then estimated the probable timing for each section.

Section	Timing (min)
·oduction	3
overview of the company	4
· analysis of Global's needs	5
ɜ features of the software	12
ɜ benefits	5
nmary	1

ch, I ate my salmon paste sandwich feeling pleased with my progress. I was happy ny structure and knew my key points and how they would be supported. However, ;offee, it occurred to me that I might not remember all my fine ideas and wonderful . I did not want a script and knew that my few slides were not going to be prompts ɜ majority of my words. I decided I needed cards.

versity I had used cards for my final (disastrous) presentation but that had failed ɹse I had tried to cram the cards with tiny words and they ended up looking like the ingredients on the back of a coke bottle. This time I decided to limit the number of ; per card to ten and give myself other useful information such as the estimated when to blank the laptop projection (using the B key), when to tell a story etc.

felt that I needed colour on my cards to help me to pick up the information quickly.

·rred to my structure and key points.

ɜd up with six cards, each $2^{1/2}$ X 4 inches:

One:

IMPACT -	UU 25% TARGET	3 MIN
NEED -	CALL-IT TESTED & PROVEN	
TIME -	30 MINUTES	PROPS
RESPONSE -	QUESTIONS AT END	
OUTLINE of STRUCTRE -		
· OVERVIEW		
· ANALYSIS		TALK SLOWLY!
· FEATURES		
· BENEFITS		

Card Two:

OVERVIEW **4 MIN**

- SINCE 1991 - HISTORY
- 500 STAFF - TYPES INCLUDE...
- LOCATIONS - DUBAI, ZURICH, BONN ETC
- HIGH PROFILE CLIENTS
- SUPPORT

SLIDE 1

TALK SLOWLY!

Card Three:

ANALYSIS 5 MIN

- MARKET GROWTH 50% P.A.
- UNIVERSAL'S GOALS
- STAFF RETENTION
- NEED FOR WORLDWIDE APPLICATION

SLIDE 2

TALK SLOWLY!

Card Four:

CALL-IT FEATURES 12 MIN

- USER FRIENDLY
- INTEGRATES ERP & BESPOKE
- PROVEN & TESTED
- MARKET LEADER

STORY

DEMONSTRATION

ard Five:

BENEFITS TO GU 5 MIN

- CROSS SELLING
- TRAINING COSTS
- DATA ACCESS & RETENTION
- SPEED

STORY

SLIDES 3/4

rd Six:

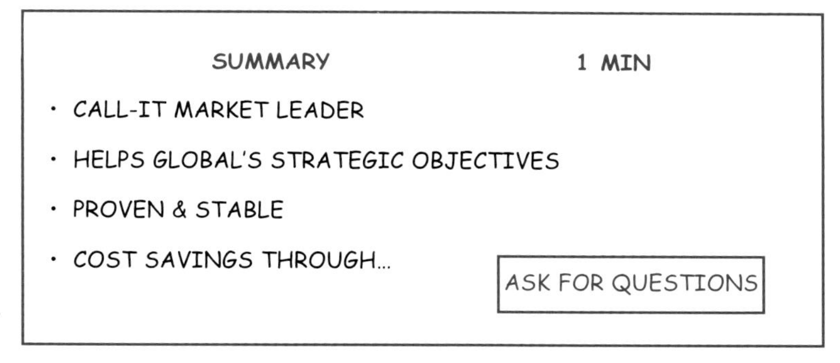

dnesday 22nd May
the completion of my cards, I felt a weight had been lifted from my mind. The antages were:

would not lose track during my presentation
had reminders about the stories, the demonstration, and the slides that ould help my speech
s I wrote them out, I clarified my key points

evening, I felt I could celebrate. So after I had put Ruth to bed, and taken more s cuttings to the tip, I had my favourite supper of salmon fish cakes accompanied by tle of Pinot Grigio. I still had a day to prepare my demonstration and few slides.

rsday 23rd May
ved early at Call-it House and within an hour I had completed my simple pictorial s and checked that my demonstration would do what I planned in the time I had ated.

As I was buying my cappuccino at the company bistro, the Caf Call-it, Jonathan Dory breezed past with the bounding Sally Bream. They were talking very loudly and seemed to have all the confidence in the world. I knew, however, from watching Sally that her confidence had evaporated when faced with an audience and she had mutated into a gibbering wreck.

The memory of Sally the presenter encouraged me to think seriously about what I shou do in my delivery.

The events of the past two weeks had caused me to concentrate on the ingredients of good communication. I had noticed the strengths and weaknesses of others like never before.

I started to note those things I should aspire to do when I got up to speak and listed the under the headings, verbal, vocal, and visual:

Verbal:
Keep the words and sentences simple
Be concise
Avoid filler words such as "erm", "actually", "absolutely", "ok" etc
Never:
Apologise
Talk down your material by saying things like "you may find this hard to read"
Ask for permission e.g. "if I may now move on to..."
Swear
Be rude
On the other hand, consider stories and appropriate humour
Say no to scripts and prepare to be flexible
Have a clear structure and ensure that key points are dealt with

Vocal:
Speak slowly
Be loud
Introduce regular, long pauses especially to reinforce my key points
Emphasise the key points
Try to be dramatic

Visual:
When the slide has served its purpose press the B key to blank the screen before continuing
As often as possible get to the front of the room and be the main focus of attention
Give 2 or 3 seconds eye contact to all members of the audience

ove calmly and smile at the audience
se gestures to show enthusiasm
can look better than I feel
e audience is not out to get me; it is in their interest for me to succeed

emembered from the intranet that if the meaning of your words is not clear, someone s estimated that about 90% of the message comes from the speaker s actions and the y they said their words. It encouraged me to believe that even if I fluffed some words it obably would not matter too much, especially because Jonathan and I would be leaving s of documentation.

wever, the thing that bothered me about my list, was how on earth I was to do all of se things and keep on speaking. It was like trying to drive a car and drive a golf ball at same time!

ecided to concentrate on one or two, and because people always said I spoke too ckly, I regarded a slow pace as my number one vocal target and eye contact to all as number one visual goal. To make sure I remembered I drew red dots (to slow down) big blue and brown eyes on my prompt cards.

t evening I practised in front of Ruth and Basil the cat. Within minutes Ruth had fallen ep and Basil became engrossed in licking himself, but at least I was able to time the very and encourage myself to speak as slowly as I could.

t night I did not sleep.

lay 24th May
oal Utilities was located on an imposing campus with a carp lake and garden in the re.

were scheduled to present at 14.00 but we arrived at 12.30. This gave us the chance ew the room beforehand and sort out the layout and equipment.

s very important for me to check the seating, the wiring, and the lighting. My decision end much of the presentation as the centre of attention meant that I needed to know e the real power point in the room was i.e. where I should stand when I blanked out lide projector. Jonathan had been taken aback by my decision not to use wall-to-wall erPoint slides, but I was determined to do it my own way. This time sorting out my rements was essential, as like my cards and my simple plan it helped my fragile dence to grow.

Shortly before our allotted time, the audience began to arrive. I was pleased with my preparations and was able to appear calm and welcoming. I pretended that this was my room and the Global team were my invited guests.- I was the host and I wanted them to be happy.

Jonathan began by introducing me and saying a few words about the company. He usec five slides during his four minutes. He handed over to me...

My first action was to blank the projector using the B key. I moved to the centre of the room and smiled at the audience.

I took my prop, a mobile phone, from my pocket
" Imagine (long pause) your customer rings to query a payment she claims was paid fc months ago (another long pause). She waits, she hears an extended list of instructions, and she hears soothing music – with luck, after three minutes she may reach a real live human voice. Alternatively she may have decided that this call is costing too much, that this firm is inefficient and cares nothing about her problem. (Pause)
She may be an ex-customer.
"Today, I shall explain how Call-it can ensure that her irritating wait would be a thing of past. (I pause, check my cards, and tell myself to slow down)
" During the next thirty minutes I will outline, firstly, a brief overview of the Call-it softwa
I will then explain how it can help Global to achieve its key customer objectives. (Pause will go on to demonstrate some of the main features of the system and then describe h it can bring cost savings through increased efficiency and customer retention.
" If you have any questions I would be delighted to hear from you at any time." (Long pause)
(Turn of first card, quick check on key parts of section one. Remind myself to smile anc talk slowly)

"How then has Call-it become the world leader in customer management? (Pause)...

"Stand still smile speak slowly pause check cards blank the screen

Speak slowly move to the centre put down the prop

Give everybody eye contact look out for nods and frowns

Pause move so everyone can see my demonstration

Speak loudly pause breathe stand still emphasise the key points

Gesture as appropriate no erms or basicallys smile oh yes, and speak!

s the talk progressed, I'm convinced I began to enjoy myself. My mind was packed with rolling sequence of self-improvement advice...
ie thirty minutes passed in a flash. My cards, my simple plan, my good start, my etermination not to rush, my simple aids supported my simple messages. As the talk ogressed, I was able to pick up the reassuring expressions from my audience.

the question and answer session after Jonathan' s talk, I was tempted to put my hands my pockets, lean on the nearest table and talk quickly, but I remembered the portance of maintaining my control. When I did not know the answer to a question I peated it or asked for clarification to buy some time. When I answered I tried to member to speak slowly and give my eye contact to all in the room and not just to the estioner.

we passed the carp pool on the way back to the car park, Jonathan said how pressed he was by my "different" approach and how it had given him pause for thought out his entirely slide-driven presentation.

nce that fateful day, my life has changed.

eem to have become addicted to the adrenaline of presenting. I now regularly present oids. I have joined the local amateur dramatic society. I have become chair of the local rdening club. I regularly ask and get the best room in hotels. I ask for discounts in ops. I always get the music turned down or changed when I am dining out, and I send ck my salmon fishcakes if they are not cooked to perfection.

n now SuperBrian.

My ten stage preparation plan:

1. Find out as much as possible about my audience
2. Write down in one sentence the purpose.

   It is always to persuade or to inform
3. Design a simple structure.

   Always including an Introduction and Summary
4. Think of likely questions
5. Write down the key points for each section
6. Decide on the timings for each section
7. Decide on what support material is needed
8. Design the prompt cards
9. Prepare the support material
10. Consider personal action points (speak slowly, eye contact etc.)

An Everyday Presentation

Lights grow dim and hearts sink low
"As you can see from slide one I m your CEO

This presentation will take you through
Our communications strategy for a year or two

If you have any questions don t bother to ask
These PowerPoint slides are up to the task

The best company brains have slaved for a week
To produce these slides and help me speak

This slide here shows lots of things
That whiz about with the occasional zing

And this one contains all sorts of stats
Produced in detail by my man Pratt

Now, these ten points explain so well
How team briefers will lecture and tell

Only thirty slides left to go
There are so many words I want to show

Here we have our new company vision
To stay alert and beat the opposition

(I hope I m not being a bore
I think someone s starting to snore)

“Oh, the screens gone blank and I ve ten slides left!
Without their help I m completely bereft

Is there anyone here who can fix this thing?
Give me some light, give IT a ring"

He gazed at the audience all vacant and drawn
No sound was heard cept the occasional yawn

He was sure they had not looked this way when he started
But PowerPoint had ensured that their souls had departed

ɿat this book was nearly called:

moved my Cheesy Wotsits?

moved my chicken soup?

moved my fish?

ɿg elephants sing

ɿg ants sing

ɿg ants and elephants dance in harmony (Teamwork in call centres)

ded Rationality and Cognitive Capabilities — a Study of Rice Collectives in North Korea

ting the Rapids

ting the Vapids

ting the Poor Performers

Age of Paradoxical Unreasonableness

Age of Something to do with the latest theory

Age of the Glittering Path (Mastering Dao-Ji)

Seven Habits of Incredible People

Seven Habits of Successful Bats

Seven (blah, blah, blah you choose)

ı Don t Buy This Book you will be a Failure!

ı Don t Buy This Book you will get Warts!

en-minute MBA

Organic Manager s Cookbook

Your Way to Senior Management

ba — A Study of why the East African tribe s successful struggle to overcome desperate omic setbacks to achieve socio-economic harmony within a diverse and sometimes e cultural environment is relevant for deprived areas of Chelsea.

ANSWERS to spurious listening exercise:

1. Second (not first!)

2. All do

3. Half way (as after that he is running OUT of the woods!)

4. One hour

5. A one pence and a ten pence piece (one is not but the other is!)

6. White (as it must be in the North Pole)

7. 70 (as 30 divided by a half is 60)

8. None. Noah built the Ark

9. Tony Blair (not the name of the Prime Minister!)

10. Your own name!

11. No as he must be dead to have a widow

ANSWERS count the fs:

There are 13 in the statement

ANSWERS hard words to spell:

Inoculate	Minuscule	Embarrass
Occurrence	Accommodate	Cemetery
Irresistible	Desiccate	Occasion
Millennium	Liaison	Weird
Supersede	Harass	Diarrhoea
Accidentally	Definitely	Ecstasy

The Appendix: Essential Medical Information

The average human brain has about 100 billion nerve cells.

Nerve impulses to and from the brain travel as fast as 170 mph. The average cough comes out of your mouth at 60 mph.

It's impossible to sneeze with your eyes open. When you sneeze, all your bc functions stop even your heart.

Your stomach needs to produce a new layer of mucus every two weeks or it would digest itself.

It takes the interaction of 72 different muscles to produce human speech.

Right handed people live, on average, nine years longer than left handed people.

Women blink nearly twice as much as men.

Blondes have more hair than dark-haired people.

The average human head weighs about 8 pounds. Our eyes are always the same size from birth, but our nose and ears never stop growing.

An average human scalp has 100,000 hairs.

The average human blinks their eyes 6,205,000 times each year.

The average surface of the human intestine is 656 square feet. The surface c the human skin is 6.5 square feet. The average human will shed 40 pounds c skin in a lifetime.

There are 45 miles of nerves in the skin of a human being.

The human heart creates enough pressure to squirt blood 30 feet. The avera heart will beat 3,000 million times in its lifetime and pump 48 million gallons c blood. Human blood travels 60,000 miles per day on its journey through the body.

During a 24-hour period, the average human will breathe 23,040 times.

Uranus has a moon called Titania and is often subjected to asteroids.